THE TIMES

Cryptic
Crossword

Book 17

Edited by Richard Browne

Published in 2013 by Times Books

HarperCollins*Publishers*
77–85 Fulham Palace Road
London W6 8JB

www.harpercollins.co.uk

1 3 5 7 9 10 8 6 4 2

© Times Newspapers Limited 2013

The Times is a registered trademark of Times Newspapers Ltd

Richard Browne asserts the moral right to be identified as the editor of this work

A catalogue record for this book is available from the British Library

ISBN 978-0-00-749167-4

Typeset by Susie Bell, www.f-12.co.uk
Printed and bound in Great Britain by Clays Ltd, St Ives plc

INTRODUCTION

Crossword compilers tend to be solitary animals, working away quietly in their own homes or gardens and communicating with their editors by email, and with their solvers by blog and tweet, if at all. But one of the considerable pleasures of compiling for *The Times* is the annual invitation to the regular core of the team to a lunch given by our appreciative Editor in London. Sometimes these lunches take place in a West End club, latterly in *The Times*'s own Wapping headquarters, with its fine top-floor views over Tower Bridge and the regenerated docks and Olympic area.

After a splendid meal, and sometimes a short talk from one of *The Times* journalists (we have heard Danny Finkelstein on what was really going on in government, and Oliver Kamm on his grandfather, the first *Times* compiler Adrian Bell), the Editor and his staff return to work and we settle down to an agreeable hour or so of discussion, involving a few points about the crossword itself, which helps to maintain the stylistic consistency we aim for. There is also much general conversation among us, many of whom are meeting again for the first time for a year.

The afternoon continues, for those without long journeys home, with a visit to a nearby pub to meet any other crossword people who are able to be there – other compilers, those who blog our efforts, other crossword editors, solvers, and general friends and relations. Then, suffused with team spirit and good wine and beer, we return home for another year of devising our fiendish tortures for you all. It's a hard life being a *Times* compiler!

Here is another collection of our crosswords, selected from those that were published during 2009, including several by Michael Curl who joined the team during the year. Puzzle 50 is a rare themed puzzle, produced for a special anniversary in September that year. I have also included all the puzzles from the Championship, which was held again at Cheltenham in October, and won again by Mark Goodliffe.

Richard Browne
January 2013

A Beginner's Guide to *The Times* Crossword

Across

1 After wrong cut, lad's looking embarrassed (7)
5 Standard of keenness of big name acting in something dirty (7)
9 Frightened, having hinted about subconscious impulses (11)
10 A bit of ballet almost finished (3)
11 Clothing sale — appeal put out for jumble (6)
12 2 — myself and my reflection? (8)
14 Is the map-room's shape changing? (13)
17 The full length of one's notice (9,4)
21 Paper's Platonic leader (8)
23 Maxim accepts English instructions for body-building (6)
25 Journey, missing time and tide (3)
26 Empty-headed husband in tears, being rejected: dirty work! (11)
27 Remove tutu for modelling (4,3)
28 Crucial stage of card game? I'm not impressed (3,4)

Down

1 Show fear of what best man carries in church (6)
2 Dispose of body? I am intervening (7)
3 One very slow European train at first stuck in tunnel (9)
4 Makes mistake, not having children? (4)
5 President needs hand with job (10)
6 Danes routed in this battle (5)
7 Makes use of cider, potentially — I tucked in (7)
8 Scatter brained, is persecuted somewhat (8)
13 With mixed feelings about the environment girl is in (10)
15 Not entirely cheerful conclusion, dropping dead at last, in the event (9)
16 In poor accommodation under a month, not one right for her (8)
18 One seeking fur turned up material piece (7)
19 Baby produces gas, having swallowed (7)
20 Time to relax on top of lounger — it helps us to nap (6)
22 Music is constant during party (5)
24 Say, stick in the post (4)

NOTES

This detailed explanation of the cluing methods for this puzzle should show you plenty of techniques (for example, some abbreviations) that are used in most of the other crosswords. I have indicated the definition elements in bold type: you will notice that virtually every clue has both a definition and a cryptic element (so these two routes to the answer should enable you to crosscheck your answer and be confident it is correct); and that the definition always comes either at the start or the end of the clue (useful tip!).

ACROSS

1   After wrong cut (CRIME, minus last letter), lad's (SON is) **looking embarrassed** (7) = CRIMSON (*is* means *this wordplay leads to the answer*)

5   **Standard of keenness** (reference to *keen as mustard*) of big name acting (STAR) in (inside) something dirty (MUD) (7) = MUSTARD (*of* means *is made up from*). Notice the pun on *acting*

9   **Frightened**, having hinted (INTIMATED) about subconscious impulses (ID – Freudian psychology) (11) = INTIMIDATED

10   **A bit of ballet** (PAS, a ballet step) almost finished (PAST, minus last letter) (3) = PAS

11   Clothing (GARB) sale — appeal put out (SA, or *sex appeal* – a common crossword conceit – is removed from SALE) for **jumble** (6) = GARBLE

12   **2** (the answer to clue 2 (down) INTERIM is the definition) — myself and my reflection? (ME and ANTI-ME!) (8) = MEANTIME

14   Is the map-room's **shape changing**? (anagram of *is the map-room's*) (13) = METAMORPHOSIS. Here, the definition and the anagram indicator are one and the same

17   **The full length of one's notice** (9,4) = ATTENTION SPAN: the whole clue is a deceptive definition, nothing to do with leaving a job!

21   **Paper's Platonic leader** (8) = GUARDIAN. Two definitions, one a reference to the Guardians who Plato recommended should be the leaders of his ideal state (if one doesn't know this classical reference, the clue is still solvable from the other definition)

23   Maxim (GNOME, a precept or pithy saying) accepts English (*English* is commonly used as code for the letter E, for which it can stand) **instructions for body-building** (6) = GENOME (the E goes inside GNOME)

25   Journey, missing time (TRIP, missing T, another common abbreviation) and **tide** (3) = RIP

26   Empty-headed (INANE) husband (H, another abbreviation) in tears (inside SNAGS), being rejected (all turned round): **dirty work!** (11) = SHENANIGANS

27   **Remove** tutu for modelling (anagram of *tutu for*) (4,3) = TURF OUT

28   **Crucial stage of card game? I'm not impressed** (3,4) = BIG DEAL (two definitions)

DOWN

1 **Show fear** of what best man carries (RING) in church (CE, another abbreviation: CH is another shorthand for *church*) (6) = CRINGE

2 Dispose of body? (INTER) I am (I'M) **intervening** (7) = INTERIM

3 **One very slow** European (E) train at first (T: this is a common way of indicating the initial letter of a word) stuck in tunnel (inside SIMPLON) (9) = SIMPLETON. A typical *Times* clue, in that the definition is not at all obvious from the wording of the clue

4 **Makes mistake**, not having children? (NO D, S – abbreviations for *daughter, son*) (4) = NODS

5 **President** needs hand (MITT) with job (ERRAND) (10) = François MITTERRAND, late President of France

6 Danes routed in **this battle** (5) = SEDAN, scene of battles in 1870, 1940; anagram of DANES

7 **Makes use of** cider, potentially (APPLES) — I tucked in (the letter "I" put inside) (7) = APPLIES

8 **Scatter** brained, is persecuted somewhat (some consecutive letters from "brained *is perse*cuted") (8) = DISPERSE. (It can be difficult to see that *scatter brained* is not to be read together; the compiler has omitted the customary hyphen, which would be unfair here)

13 **With mixed feelings** about the environment (AMBIENT) girl is in (VAL inside) (10) = AMBIVALENT

15 Not entirely cheerful (HAPPY, without its final Y) conclusion (ENDING), dropping dead at last (taking off the last letter of *dead*, D), in the event (9) = HAPPENING

16 In poor accommodation (GARRET) under a month (MAR, abbreviation for *March*), not one right (R stands for *right*, and we must find one of the Rs to remove) for **her** (8) = MARGARET

18 **One seeking fur** turned up (reversed the letters of) material (REP, a ribbed fabric) piece (PART) (7) = TRAPPER

19 **Baby** produces gas (NEON), having swallowed (ATE) (7) = NEONATE

20 Time (T) to relax (EASE) on top of lounger (L) — **it helps us to nap** (6) = TEASEL (a prickly flower-head used to raise a nap)

22 **Music** is (IS) constant (C) during party (inside DO) (5) = DISCO

24 Say, stick (JAM, which sounds the same) in **the post** (4) = JAMB

THE PUZZLES

1

ACROSS

1 Report firearms having been stolen (7)
5 Copying tragic heroine, shed tears (7)
9 Seven are DIY fans, and don't give up hope (5,3,3)
10 Butter or batter (3)
11 Frightened with frequency during an attack (6)
12 Brothers sort of singing at opening of Italian wine (8)
14 Little tremors are unimportant (2,5,6)
17 Building with wooden floor assembled in Tennessee (5,2,6)
21 North African man embracing German one (8)
23 Imprisoned in Kabul, I acquire pathological indecisiveness (6)
25 Drink a peg by the sound of it (3)
26 One taking wrong direction round Cooperative (6,5)
27 Curtailed visit finishes at beginning of month (7)
28 Feeling dizzy on horseback, attempt to get horse moving (5-2)

DOWN

1 Friendly greetings expressed nicely in any language right from the start (6)
2 Northern Ireland runs a delivery service, turning up in a stew (7)
3 Hurrying, captures bishop and then queen — a sign of things to come (9)
4 Split up rock (4)
5 Remove restrictions after doctor shows restraint (10)
6 Encounters rising respect after decapitation (5)
7 Fish leads vessel into designated area (3,4)
8 Clock us — my time is most gratifying (8)
13 Carnivores found in 17 (10)
15 Narrow-minded scoundrel takes in one young girl (9)
16 Small network occupying top floor, in the main (8)
18 Bird with silver back (7)
19 Dispersed fully in void (7)
20 About to draw breath, pulled up to drop off (6)
22 Without going to extremes, establishing cost of castor-oil product (5)
24 Call round (4)

ACROSS

1   Stout assistance needed for such a comfortably-settled cat, nevertheless! (4-6)
6   Speed restriction makes little impact (4)
8   Breeding establishment quiet following a feeding concern (4-4)
9   Nothing on reflection stops bore sending document (6)
10 Cross when young Australian skipper departs (4)
11 Without completed book, novelist is unfairly treated (4-4-2)
12 Three couples' success overwhelmed (3,3,3)
14 Grant after start of spying given to spook (5)
17 Scottish town making bread without taxing people (5)
19 Stunning lean ox stewed with pig (9)
22 To fake death in asylum, Pop's mad (4,6)
23 Work to an extent messes up one's back (4)
24 Appropriate greeting card (6)
25 Badge one gains in manoeuvres (8)
26 Drive odd characters away from Aztec site (4)
27 Mainly abandoned Test team getting cross (6-4)

DOWN

1   Unconvincing knight follows convulsed with fear (5-4)
2   Survive as the only solicitor in Louisiana? (4,3)
3   Wary about new hat but like old boots? (8)
4   Artist in shelter? Men stand out in all weather (4,4,2,5)
5   Welshman's rage upset second of my daughters (6)
6   Timeshare package with director on board (3,3,3)
7   Rule stipulating modest dress cooler for hotel guest? (7)
13 Personally found variable gin uplifting (3,2,4)
15 Bloke upset unusually large ladies and old country folk (9)
16 Showed the setter a reflective comment (3,2,3)
18 Such records make me dance with a lilt (3-4)
20 Urge to embrace a new recruit to jury (7)
21 Explorer getting energy after eating one? (6)

ACROSS

1 Drug dealer maybe whose rates are high? (5,8)
8 Film has a lot to say (4)
9 Copy is pre-Art Deco reproduction (4-6)
10 German ship with British monarch at the helm (8)
11 Piece of music sung regularly at church (6)
13 Heading out of film studio, Disney seen round part of Manhattan (4,6)
16 Tackle lecherous sort (4)
17 Approaching target with rifle? (4)
18 "Hate list" you'd returned includes two kinds of record (10)
20 Disease, one repeatedly eradicated from North Africa (6)
22 Sugary shortbread's first served with tiny pieces of this (8)
24 Such rude humour disconcerted a rival a lot (10)
26 Caligula for one lost his heart to a horse (4)
27 Fish finger (half portion) with bread eaten at front of pier (6,7)

DOWN

1 Organise male celebrity's rise over time (5-6)
2 Support to reduce stress on learner (5)
3 Set off from school wearing old hat (9)
4 Extra PE ordered for one side (2,5)
5 Kids seen without right sort of trousers (5)
6 Bridge over top of underground station in foreign port (9)
7 One sails on sea or lake briefly (3)
12 Follows new course, having got together a pile of cash? (7,4)
14 Nelly found garment in flashy fabric cool (9)
15 Dug underground passage, adjusted to accommodate little girl (9)
19 Writer rejecting interference over article he saves (7)
21 For starters, raspberries in orange juice with a wine from Spain (5)
23 Sort out old trunk (5)
25 Great king briefly carried by palfrey (3)

4

ACROSS

1 Legendary ship queen's boarded before now (4)
3 This is unusual in Panama's border, say — it's a UK thing (10)
10 Where letters are usually found to be concise (2,1,4)
11 Punish chaps engaged in wrongdoing (7)
12 Tudors in Tunics, a reworking for this play? (5,10)
13 Planet was located in front of vessel (6)
14 Not crazy about introduction of Chardonnay, slip in another wine (8)
17 Distressed pair in need to put on a brave face? (3,5)
18 Noisily overwhelm most of lifeless wetland (6)
21 Crushing this could produce red dye or Catholic incense (9,6)
23 English seabird beside a lake unchanged by time (7)
24 Someone out of breath catching hot leopard (7)
25 Change of form involving harm, mostly (10)
26 Belgian songwriter regularly seen in bordello (4)

DOWN

1 Drunk and knight are upstanding toffs (7)
2 Sailor crowned by soldier, perhaps several, gets a big shiner (5,4)
4 Nibbler traversed nudist's extremities (6)
5 Teaching session worked out in test (8)
6 Second group nabbed by officer with preference for annual tidy-up (6-8)
7 Bile accumulates in part of an intestinal section (5)
8 Painter lifted heart of chesty model in the morning (7)
9 A minor exchange could make it appropriate to chat about maintenance (14)
15 Top-up course concerning new student (9)
16 Dim military subdivision surrounding French from both sides (8)
17 Roughly hew my hollow lilac tree (4,3)
19 Uncultivated part of South Africa once including ancient city … (7)
20 … another one, very quiet, with a sign on the outskirts (6)
22 Sign on staff with time divided (5)

ACROSS

1 Land in America and disperse (6)
5 Make flattering comments in indulgent TV programme (4-4)
9 Service problems resulting from crossed lines (4,6)
10 Time excluded from world records, unfortunately (4)
11 News about maiden taken to court produces bitterness (8)
12 Articles carried by French priest (6)
13 Old-fashioned art, for example, in extremely short book (4)
15 Depositing about a thousand, so making charges (8)
18 Besides, you can continue on the next page (8)
19 Lied as child before finally confessing (4)
21 Facial protection for a tree-feller (6)
23 Combine around NATO member in determined way (8)
25 Clue that produces suspicion (4)
26 Celebrities not altogether complimentary about new title (10)
27 Bossy old woman's husband I had seen in Scottish island (8)
28 Don't like being put in post again (6)

DOWN

2 Touchy and old, under pressure, snap (5)
3 In English firm, I'm worthy of deep respect (9)
4 One churchman or another holding firm (6)
5 Disaster one can't blame on other party (4-11)
6 Quickly dispatched rations for the fleet? (4,4)
7 Jump off (5)
8 Greek king, soon securing match, married (9)
14 Mysteries, including a secret I spread around inner circle (9)
16 Kills rival after service (9)
17 Declare antique, having done statistical calculation (8)
20 Vessel, say, south of cape (6)
22 Make overt change, as supporter of politician (5)
24 Translating from this language? Just the opposite (5)

6

Across

1 Old gun in church in Derbyshire town (9)
6 Young child missing final drama in cartoon film (5)
9 At end of declaration sign name in classical style (5)
10 Watching amount eaten by Russian runner (9)
11 Inside the car the Queen waves (7)
12 King's man attached to company, facing army in revolution? (7)
13 I've delirium and it's somehow producing an apparent reality (14)
17 Such is eNORMously outstanding leader! (8-6)
21 Small place with comforts and delights (7)
23 Provincial group in charge of African people (7)
25 Canon has gold ball stuck outside home (9)
26 Law handed down here: offence attracts fine (5)
27 Valley with moderate climate lacking merit (5)
28 Workers given fish as introductory offer? (9)

Down

1 Fellow to crawl out of lake, one that's swamped? (8)
2 Language used by almost a million (5)
3 Resentment splitting husband and maybe young male dependants (7-2)
4 Animal work leads to very big money (7)
5 Ship crossing strait followed by river bird (7)
6 Brought up without love and disaffected (5)
7 Men in deal — I'm out to get right purchasing system (4,5)
8 Bars offering foul stingo (6)
14 Man who's wicked and deranged turning up in port (9)
15 Supports in bays perhaps to hold shelf up (9)
16 Number in favour of corporal punishment given a hearing (8)
18 The drink? More than one sailor in this is lost (7)
19 Uncongenial accommodation gets muck over time (7)
20 Shoot something for Christmas dinner? (6)
22 Only one not left with superficial injury (5)
24 Country knight wearing classical attire (5)

ACROSS

1 Sack belonging to Parisian model (6)
4 Possibly don church vestment mostly worn by old rebel (8)
10 Furniture maker's quiet demise amidst food and drink (11)
11 Time to abandon street fighting in old capital (3)
12 Like an old tribesman chosen, say, by his organisation (7)
14 Constant bearing (7)
15 Point made by PM repeatedly changing seat (5-5-4)
17 Girl shortly lined up for dissembling (14)
21 Egocentric son's angle on the Spanish (7)
22 Cat the writer's kept in quarters (7)
23 Profit pursued, ignoring the odds (3)
24 Painful condition that may result from intense blow (6,5)
26 Huge farm implements dislodging 1,000 small bones (8)
27 Opening a girl found in key transport system (6)

DOWN

1 Dodge school, going round new swimming facility (4-4)
2 Foreign character's expression of distaste for listeners (3)
3 Rising RAF officers accompanying aircraft designer (7)
5 Typical letters about current nervous affliction (14)
6 Where in Scotland children once raised fish (7)
7 Metal tool damaging limes in park (11)
8 Crow making sound of steam engine, say (6)
9 Cricket sides fall out, carrying article in case (2,3,3,6)
13 Head with soft drink shows affability … (11)
16 … subject to method making progress (5,3)
18 Senseless disdain regularly concerning the listener? (7)
19 Unskilled ship's officer visiting a Babylonian city (7)
20 Somehow does without copper coin (6)
25 Prohibit financial institution going short (3)

Across

1   Take attitude you can find accommodation inside old tavern (3-5)
5   Manual rewritten for Harvard graduate (6)
9   Film director has collar with tight fastening (8)
10 Remain cheerful, as Godiva in Coventry was said to be (4,2)
12 Part most enthusiastically received (5)
13 Advantage gained ultimately by top performer in contest (4,5)
14 Decline of old civilisation makes one very angry (12)
18 Sceptics observe Lenin agitating (3-9)
21 Amazingly lithe hare, less prone to disease (9)
23 Bird left to sulk outside (5)
24 Wandering terrier finally tethered by a rope (6)
25 Shoelace fastened, say, as ordered (6,2)
26 In insurrection, taking a chance king will be deposed (6)
27 Inactive family member with little time for men at first (8)

Down

1   Vegetable dish served with salt cod quite regularly (6)
2   Mostly constant worker? Hardly (6)
3   Possibility detective will replace one in position of authority (3-6)
4   Revealed chap has changed appearance in weird sci-fi musical (5,7)
6   Team is top of the league, it's announced (5)
7   Woman about to visit seaside resort briefly (8)
8   Laid up, old man has little desire for food (8)
11 Deliver daily paper going round island quickly (4,4,4)
15 Boy band secures tour (9)
16 Unsettled when travelling by plane (2,3,3)
17 Royal females mostly dreamt of? (8)
19 Cleric in nave held up a religious effigy (6)
20 Don't pose for artist without a shirt (4,2)
22 Tutor put up pictures of Belfast, perhaps (5)

ACROSS

1 Kind of cheese for a sad mood? (4,4)
5 Term of modification braved somehow (6)
9 Old copper used in standard valve (8)
10 Chanted words reduced danger to trespassers (6)
12 Morality play to uplift all of us (5,3,4)
15 Oxygen has obstinate pervasive quality (5)
16 Press sure to be inflexible (9)
18 Conductor taking opera to province repeatedly (9)
19 American maturity custom (5)
20 Entertainer whose fans await his forthcoming release? (12)
24 Pass out with start of ill-health's return (6)
25 Muse needs a little time inside to intervene helpfully (8)
26 It's sharper for one lamenting (6)
27 For me, easiest to travel about one (2,1,3,2)

DOWN

1 Stud manager (4)
2 British diplomats in America — they're out of this world! (4)
3 Vicars ordered to welcome the first lady opposite (4,5)
4 Ricer boiling madly is now beyond redemption (12)
6 Heading off internal rising showing some tension (5)
7 More painting required in college department (10)
8 Comedy hero shortage during British summer (10)
11 I sit by lake — such grandeur! (12)
13 Constriction of nerve on part of body (10)
14 Scene actor played, giving cause to be respected (10)
17 Berlin's air conducive to original thought? (4,5)
21 Lawmen have final vessel removed (5)
22 Get smaller cart, say (4)
23 Clothing son in check (4)

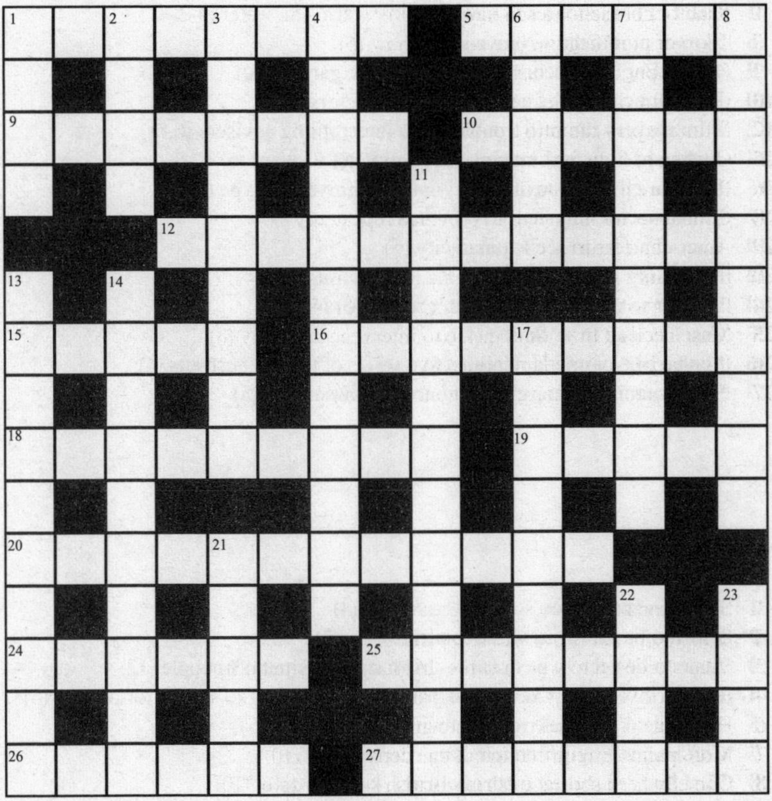
1
2
3
4
5
6
7
8
9
10
11
12
13
14
15
16
17
18
19
20
21
22
23
24
25
26
27

ACROSS

1 Habit of old labourer to have to drink warm salt water (4-2-4)
6 Skewer points the wrong way (4)
9 Grand English celebrities recalled in the garden (10)
10 Ruler appearing before twelve tax collectors (4)
12 Film makers run into trouble when interrupting advisers (6,8)
14 Awkward high ball moving backward, not forward (6)
15 Reliable chap following angry-looking university type (8)
17 Film director, unusually, is TV icon (8)
19 Runs charters to see Russian city (6)
22 Hurt using pins (7,7)
24 Statesman once put round letter with flyer (4)
25 One has lead to walk dog (4-6)
26 Maybe like painter's retrospective series of twenty portraits (4)
27 Small mammal emerging from tree throws nuts (5,5)

DOWN

1 What ends with you solving the Jumbo (4)
2 Sport to be arranged with female boxing (7)
3 Time to be seen in posh car — Mini strangely put off people (12)
4 Patient investigator keeps one grounded, beginning to search for objects (6)
5 More bleak land one refuses to give up (8)
7 City buried English couple after ceremony (7)
8 First Lady launched fresh take-over, keeping quiet (10)
11 Sticking quality grub up by natural lake (12)
13 One disappearing from sight in a cruiser solvent again (5,5)
16 Monitor elderly relative getting in way, not moving (8)
18 Separate and better info was illuminating (5,2)
20 Speaker has little cutting to say when leader is away (7)
21 Officer's superior to take this fuse (6)
23 Raffle is very attractive event (4)

ACROSS

1   Cut back on expensive clothes, primarily, and start to knit a sweater (4,4)
5   A motel owner screened moderates (6)
9   Show record (8)
10 Work left over, too much for musicians (6)
12 Dreamy court official's last to join congregation (4-9)
15 One newspaper in US city that's smart (5)
16 This might account for booze being found on allotment (9)
17 Disasters — naturally — in light lingerie (9)
19 Lexicographer not getting on with man behind Biggles (5)
20 A supporter is supposed to talk informally, having formerly popped in (8,5)
22 Disinfectant fluid no help? (6)
23 Little woman getting letters from a minor artist (4,4)
25 Change for member of youth group once provided with ultimate in finery (6)
26 Species that is protected while sea is regulated (3,5)

DOWN

1   Blue gastropod (10)
2   Record kept of fuel consumed (3)
3   Reportedly, has taped jolly posy (7)
4   Keeping seat vacant, inspirit all competitors with somewhere to sit (12)
6   Mexican dish, in a manner of speaking, one has to finish (7)
7   A proper Goth is revolting — he ought to know his place (11)
8   Work as a farrier in Oxford, for example (4)
11 Winding streets to a single male driver? (12)
13 Cap in hand is so deranged (3,4,4)
14 Divine queen, essentially mobile, perhaps (10)
18 Attention seeker curtly announcing close of play? (4-3)
19 Like Aristides, won over a little while ago (4,3)
21 Draw up plans for unwanted delivery (4)
24 Reduced state of princess on stage (3)

ACROSS

1 Man in church taking Prior's pew hard to dislodge (10)
6 Measure of insulation given by a draped cloth (4)
8 As trader, I have role in *Macbeth* (8)
9 One beaten in test twice coming back (3-3)
10 Sellers for example are persistent (4)
11 Woman from fashionable part of London without a title (2,4,4)
12 Good book, one in final English edition for kids … (9)
14 … children's author is shortly back for another (5)
17 Love to visit women, confined here? (5)
19 Bird wants part of crocus, or insect (9)
22 City kid is hot stuff (10)
23 Endless gaze — up at this? (4)
24 Country controlled by British? That's over (6)
25 Magic figure mustn't start to be confusing (8)
26 Pretty short flower for border (4)
27 From ancestors to present time covered in record (10)

DOWN

1 Complaining of joint in limb (9)
2 Fighting — poor ref gets blame (7)
3 Not late round at friend (8)
4 Series of jobs as artist? (9,6)
5 Afterwards turning up to hold one sort of sale (6)
6 City entrance has church and pub (6,3)
7 Northerner's extremely gruesome alternative to do? (7)
13 How daffodils appeared to Wordsworth: neat, local arrangement (3,2,4)
15 Tony failed to overcome right-wingers' endless bad reputation (9)
16 Crushed, mischief-maker behaved unnaturally (8)
18 Song by crow in the past, a busy flier (7)
20 Caribbean island, as opposed to Pacific one miles away (7)
21 Book is excellent — what a surprise! (6)

13

ACROSS

1   National newspaper (8)
6   Old measure protecting son of modern artist (6)
9   Miss a festive occasion (4)
10   Audibly disapproving of pet vocation (10)
11   Place of worship in which a celebrant gets excited (10)
13   Choice of week-ends for function (4)
14   Limit my development with new movie stand-ins (8)
16   A U-bend, unusual in river (6)
18   Chicken caught by another bird (6)
20   Residing, unfortunately, in location near fighting (8)
22   Murder victim a blow prematurely ended (4)
24   A frolic in a drunken state (10)
26   Stop a bid to limit old-fashioned theatrical fan-worship (10)
28   Art patron from Central America? (4)
29   Musician in film, on piano (6)
30   Antonio, say, makes me run and sing repeatedly (8)

DOWN

2   Part I, for example (9)
3   Work out about 50% deal for this? (5-2)
4   Wine servant passed around company (5)
5   Final score (3)
6   Type name included by college fellow (9)
7   Tory leader barely achieved victory (7)
8   So-called foreign gentleman somebody's raised right (5)
12   Most important, like this answer (7)
15   Colour man got wrong, having limited vision (9)
17   One sport in place of another (9)
19   Very friendly type concealing identity in lawful way (7)
21   Withdraw money (7)
23   Noisily show emotion about boxer's last fight (5)
25   Quickly move queen or rook, for example (5)
27   Male to male bonding (3)

ACROSS

1 Excited with container for drawers to cover furniture (9)
6 Those in circus seeing assistant's backflip on to magician's head (5)
9 Various extraordinary people worship Him (7)
10 Very little to inspire in parting tresses on top of toupee (4,3)
11 Outline suggestion (5)
12 As The Invisible Man's wandering continued? (9)
13 Pretence in government department one might rumble as junior official (8)
14 Musical direction taken in familiar concerti (4)
17 Drug addict leaves torchbearer disheartened (4)
18 Out beyond this, mean business (8)
21 Affair that's horrid's ending marriage (9)
22 Smoke one's beginning to get between wheels (5)
24 Are brothers so organised? (2,5)
25 Allow room for a garden in spring (4,3)
26 English composer's written about in flier (5)
27 Leader knowing a couple of names in Norfolk town (5,4)

DOWN

1 Surprise result, winning place (5)
2 Properly assembled furniture shouldn't appear unstable (4,1,5,5)
3 One observes fool hugging fair Queen (6-2)
4 Uprising revealed decay, with America involved (8)
5 Portly about fatty's middle? (6)
6 Part that is in witty remark, with funny ending (6)
7 In a war, ideal guy to restore captured vehicle to the road (4,11)
8 Where one might land a fee, ultimately, stick with capital (9)
13 Child left unfolding plaits (9)
15 Nameless rogue traders (8)
16 Sweet items with treacly centre stuffed into pockets (8)
19 Problem to sort out (6)
20 Protection from the wet geek (6)
23 Something shining over material (5)

ACROSS

1 Assumed spies engaged in airlift at sea (10)
6 Attempt from bunker, initially with wood (4)
10 A Greek starter (5)
11 Lover in Italian city turned over at end of siesta (9)
12 Content sot, very drunk, deliberately ignored by everyone (4,2,8)
14 Careful in plant close to machinery (7)
15 Arousing intense feeling in English grounds (7)
17 Cars in residential areas (7)
19 Adept, old lady's secured role (7)
20 Head after those who flogged cheeky kid (14)
23 Flipping angry, chasing cad in port (9)
24 Furious, marauder at sea losing power (5)
25 A fish out of water gulping oxygen (4)
26 Writer's book, hit, one adding fuel to the fire (4,6)

DOWN

1 A girl has bottom pinched, unfortunately (4)
2 Classified operations on Crete, possibly after onset of terrorism (3-6)
3 Snaps the toffee into pieces for Boxing Day (5,2,7)
4 Smart Conservative heading off for plant (7)
5 Sailor, with no one else present, produces seafood (7)
7 A fraction to one side (5)
8 But not the sort of music you'd associate with steel or brass bands? (5,5)
9 Reach the headland and stop rambling (4,2,3,5)
13 People generally in support of different afterlife (5,5)
16 Lacking information during the night? (2,3,4)
18 Frodo's pony showing pace on runs (7)
19 In short skirt, mother's bottom (7)
21 Bury's season without foremost of wingers (5)
22 Get to know, briefly, a humorist (4)

ACROSS

1 Retail decision made — I'm extending credit (3,3,4)
6 Fine political party that's often fought (4)
10 Chop I wash, removing an area of dead skin (7)
11 The last in a series of disasters that's left by building workers (3,4)
12 Advise leftie to keep remark short (9)
13 In town, the carpet-maker is … (5)
14 Old civilisation the founder of another backed (5)
15 Extremely silly show without initial backers (9)
17 Epic drama involved emergency worker (9)
20 Discharge about to be reversed? Capital! (5)
21 Cursing, catching horse with crop (5)
23 React badly to sugary confection, say — it keeps coming back (9)
25 Left a section without many words (7)
26 Style of art in which silver's applied to new figure (7)
27 Composer, not one to cloy (4)
28 Implores to move to London, say (10)

DOWN

1 Become responsible for terminal, and able to depart (5)
2 Perhaps one held up to ridicule at last calmer after explosion (9)
3 Strange — millions gifted to firm (14)
4 Hero's academic works captivated university (7)
5 A tot in short queue for kids' show (7)
7 Spread out neatly in gift boxes (5)
8 Wretched people come to a district in Ireland (9)
9 Silly fuss damages important cause (5,2,1,6)
14 Classical versifier filled parts of feet with power — this in Latin (9)
16 Clear-out opening space to display Raphael, say (9)
18 Disaster as class make up for time lost in discussion (7)
19 Dog taking up colourful soup (7)
22 In a series of races champion has no part to play (5)
24 Part of the family giving news to us (5)

ACROSS

1 Vegetables I stuffed into metal container that doesn't close (9)
6 Maybe watch broadcast about middle of afternoon (5)
9 A Côtes-du-Rhone — good little number — cellared here? (7)
10 Snare has component with handle that won't stop turning (7)
11 Appeal to Liberal, in a manner of speaking (5)
12 Check made by tutor during break (9)
14 Woman moaned regularly (3)
15 Dog given tail of fish you caught (6,5)
17 Photograph fearsome women in bloomers (11)
19 Hear shot (3)
20 Lights a source of torment for sea creature (4,5)
22 That is part of bride's trousseau (2,3)
24 Complaining vehicle has a metallic sound (7)
26 Stop working, currently wanting holiday abroad (4,3)
27 A good deal resting on launch of Daily Sketch (5)
28 One who celebrates distribution of gay report (9)

DOWN

1 Dull British countryside (5)
2 Fire a colleague, bringing new one in (7)
3 Clergyman's estate in foreign province provides somewhere to sleep (6,3)
4 Secret agent sent out where the action is (6,5)
5 Dishonest scheme hasn't caught him? (3)
6 Several men following course (5)
7 Manchester United's outside right, number one scorer (7)
8 Journalist going after position in bank, according to general belief (9)
13 Cheers top player, almost out early, surprisingly (3,3,5)
14 Several weeks stuck on mountains I'm climbing, lost (9)
16 Soldiers landed within Italy's frontiers, showing warlike attitude (9)
18 More relaxed after heading off, I'll reach a Spanish resort (7)
19 Artist's link with explorer (7)
21 Change dress (5)
23 Russian fighters twice meeting resistance (5)
25 Doctor binds a fracture (3)

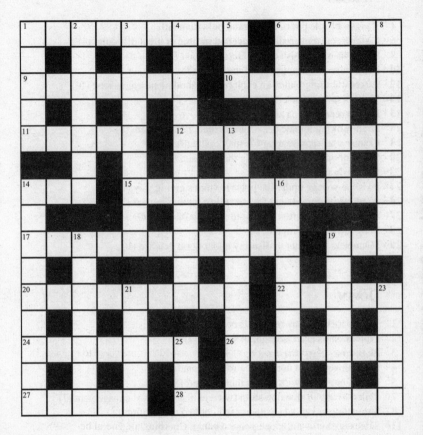

ACROSS

1 Reagan people put in for a grand politician (10)
6 Oxford's current credit is cancelled in time of great difficulty (4)
9 Pompous old rubbish and in German, too (7)
10 Support record amount piled in in-tray (7)
12 Acknowledging faults, an explorer has good name going west (10)
13 Spoil is soil with a letter missing (3)
15 Layout representing abridged book (6)
16 High-ranking female prisoner returned valuable item (8)
18 Colour a set representing Cornish castle (8)
20 Sailor good on virtue? Totally the opposite (6)
23 Regularly take repast (3)
24 Possible voyage under the polar ice that's giving way (10)
26 Am I into natural talent for a relaxing type of music? (7)
27 Leaves a church after deliberate slanting of views (7)
28 Song top E's interrupted? (4)
29 Financiers have met in disarray about flood defence (10)

DOWN

1 What's locked away in Carisbrooke castle (4)
2 Professionals exercise right to succeed (7)
3 Be bilious, alas, stirring soup (13)
4 I add nitrogen and use a spade round plant (6)
5 Lambs bite lions with this in their hearts? (8)
7 Sailor wrong to abandon stern twice in historic naval engagement (7)
8 Something sweet, saucy and grand cooked up (5,5)
11 Sidecars, say — mark one going through Cheshire? (8,5)
14 Berliners once had to keep this American eccentric (3,3,4)
17 Girl got round bachelor chap with those exact words (8)
19 Important person that's never a dummy? (7)
21 Raised fabric which might have been woven to be a cord (7)
22 Oppressive atmosphere created by girl's mother (6)
25 It's something to put son on really attractive photo (4)

18

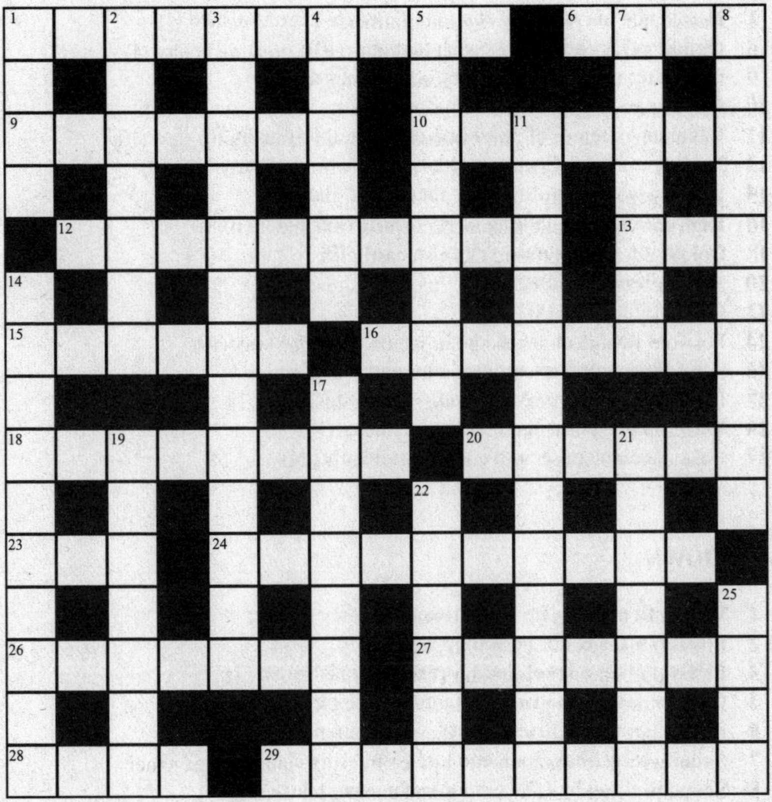

ACROSS

1 Heroic tale the writer of *Bonjour Tristesse* left unfinished (4)
4 Childhood friend taking coach to match (10)
9 Composer reportedly bitten by scoundrel's dog (10)
10 Good years regularly yielding flowing water (4)
11 Ultimate extremes of upset doctors treated originally (6)
12 Northern chap in Cockney's house, one who'll eat anything (8)
14 Solitary workman ultimately abandoned plant (4)
15 Low vehicle with nothing on it running over pole? (10)
17 Old prison mother must visit, some say (10)
20 Select players for fling (4)
21 Girl enthralled by 007? (8)
23 A Greek character twice identifying an Egyptian god (6)
24 Girl in black perhaps secured husband (4)
25 Decorative lantern a Moor oddly misused (10)
26 Retired PM's point about unknown dozer (10)
27 National emblem seen to collapse suddenly? (4)

DOWN

2 It's drunk in a day, up to the time of a party (11)
3 Possibly she's at our bookshop signing (9)
4 Doubter takes a lot of flak for pinching mushroom (7)
5 One may accommodate aspirants, to a degree (4,2,9)
6 39 books were sufficient for an old Roman port (7)
7 Sound young Shakespearean lord dismissing clan leaders? (5)
8 Lofty dwelling built by first of yachtsmen in lake (5)
13 Bring round cruets — tea is prepared (11)
16 Short walk in no state to be used after dark (9)
18 Physical structure of a cat in a US city (7)
19 Given a turn, as a door handle may be? (7)
21 Phoney press employee accepts advance, given rise (5)
22 Egg on soldiers making gunpowder ingredient (5)

20

ACROSS

1 Unfair trying to link good chap in power with bounder (8,7)
9 A girl the different clubs become reluctant to move (9)
10 Roughly gatecrashing inn back in Lancashire town (5)
11 Martial art mostly random hit and miss (6)
12 Like to eat rubbish endlessly — and seafood (8)
13 You may underperform, portrayed as heartless operatic heroine (3,3)
15 London park and thoroughfare very untidy when judge visits (2,6)
18 Countered blows to the ear, finding a safe place (4,4)
19 Grand American cheers very small Swede, perhaps (6)
21 In Ireland my drinks are spiked with punch (8)
23 Old actor not allowing women to go with leading lady (6)
26 Speaker may appeal to class (5)
27 Short Mystery plays in verse an official found in church (9)
28 Like one driven through entrance, far from quick! (4,2,1,4-4)

DOWN

1 Extremely kindly, wrapping ailing Jack with old wet blanket (7)
2 Famous tree oddly bathed in green light (5)
3 It's smart killing a creature that's hard to catch (1,4,4)
4 Lower head in blood-soaked riot (4)
5 One in rising company stops German's agreed influence (8)
6 One seeing future is reflecting on past line (5)
7 Acting together on stage? (2,7)
8 Does out old naval officer's quarters (7)
14 Run Jamaica rum — caught dropping drug (9)
16 One putting energy into X-rated sin? (9)
17 What cattle go through, circling near African city (8)
18 I forbid tearing of tissue (7)
20 Driver on a landau keeping one in a draught? (7)
22 UK carrier bags inflamed Dutch town (5)
24 A bit of Greek language book never gets right (5)
25 Who speculates will also ultimately generate capital (4)

ACROSS

1 Being partly able to forgive his other half's errors? (7)
5 Brains shown by bachelor in strange career (7)
9 No-win situation, even though some goals were achieved (5,4)
10 Money for memorial in church (5)
11 Part of what's eaten on cruise, for example (2,3)
12 Make impact with a lot of money up front for big contract (5,4)
14 Unusual asset still seen in material that resists corrosion (9,5)
17 Payment to state resulting from certain things of which Twain spoke? (11,3)
21 Roughly treat German author and composer in speech (9)
23 From every other part of Africa, cram back into one of its capitals (5)
24 Result of bulb being wrongly lit up (5)
25 Old painter has to prepare canvas, covering it, I see (9)
26 Rider's unyielding, restraining a gee-gee (7)
27 Intelligence chief with one of his men before a battle (7)

DOWN

1 Hits I had taken, knocked over, black and blue (6)
2 Doctor filming disappearance of satellite (7)
3 Soldier making the most of tropical island? That's right (9)
4 Changed, eg, dated rule? (11)
5 Sound made by rook, out of its throat (3)
6 Crazy attack with bishop in centre (5)
7 Educator who produced outstanding characters (7)
8 Diet, perhaps, for start of day at school (8)
13 Being out of one's class in semis, beaten badly (11)
15 Notices one part of house going up and down (9)
16 Maiden is lighter in unequal contest (8)
18 Support lost by ass given endless talking-to (4,3)
19 Sale you announced, in case (7)
20 Male paid to attend a dance (6)
22 Dominant leader in Athens, originally (5)
25 Under pressure, get commercial protection for member (3)

ACROSS

1   Pitch in when leader abandons string player (6)
4   Badly written about — in story apt to err (8)
10 Historic region of China — Amur running here (9)
11 Bill has no time for puzzle (5)
12 Not quite making a claim about love-in-a-mist (7)
13 Former journalists not stopping newspaper, say (7)
14 Two notes identifying conductor (5)
15 Implements in America mostly capable of being stretched (8)
18 Mad dog heard in an Irish port (8)
20 Man of La Mancha not beginning card game (5)
23 Medicine was our common bond, we hear (7)
25 Animal for which Spooner may have had money back (3,4)
26 Half a month left for literary work (5)
27 Sinatra sang this to the end (3,3,3)
28 Dear seen playing composition (8)
29 Laid up in Dorset resort (6)

DOWN

1   Warn a good-looking person about first day at work, perhaps (8)
2   The French inheritance ascendant in former French colony (7)
3   Old Viennese piece by Strauss, initially scary (9)
5   Usually emulate Franco? (2,1,7,4)
6   Delight in friend coming over at university (3,2)
7   Primarily, biographer of Samuel, wonderfully eccentric Lichfield lexicographer (7)
8   Pick up material seconds after departure (6)
9   Tale of adventure and natural desires at sea (8,6)
16 Part of fruit not eaten by rabbit or bird (9)
17 Punt a couple of chaps sold down the river (8)
19 Exceed time allotted for review (3,4)
21 African conflict in which fighter loses heart, turning green (4,3)
22 Flora schemes to have central heating installed (6)
24 Hooker from Catalonia (5)

ACROSS

1 What's needed for one being sick on street? (9)
6 Tree seen in mist at length (5)
9 Girl is after good measure of wine (5)
10 Departs East Anglian town — about time, having control of car (3,6)
11 Film no actor could make? (8,7)
13 Very important to keep united? I don't think so, for foreign Protestant (8)
14 Irritating beetle? (6)
16 Roof needs clean top, but not edges (4-2)
18 Emergency rations in camp: mine need cooking (8)
21 Film director ad-libs the moves around set (4-11)
23 I chuck in uninteresting fossil (9)
25 That's posh, a name for Welshman (5)
26 Get ready to open state prison (5)
27 Clever chap parrots note about heroin and speed (4,5)

DOWN

1 Greek character drops temperature in part of plant (5)
2 Going through book, girl admits love to be theme of ballad (7,4)
3 Opera, like, heartless? That's relatively accurate (2,5)
4 Line of trees chap would propagate round either side of estate (8)
5 Put record in to storage container and tidy cases (6)
6 Writers' village has endless value (7)
7 Spot instrument woman's dropped (3)
8 Opera is long, with her in cast (9)
12 Glass to repack here? Time to work (6,5)
13 9 may stand up (4,5)
15 Delivery one turns away (3-5)
17 Secure sort of house to have (3,4)
19 Like girl's mother, one beauty (7)
20 A cut closes university hall (6)
22 Old invader grasps top of cannon ball (5)
24 Troublemaker every constituency has? (3)

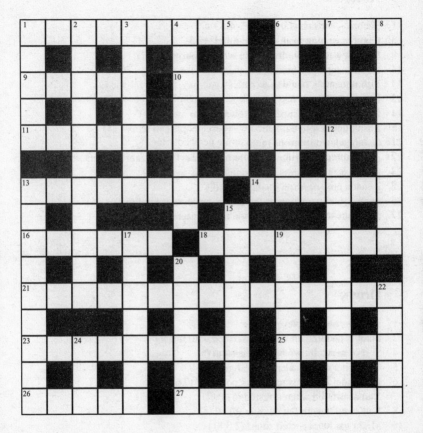

ACROSS

1 Second — which is irritating! (4)
3 Good reasoning from a stable mind? (5,5)
9 Son allowed out on drugs, one wrote mournfully (7)
11 Release copy in a month, not the first (7)
12 Fish returning, one way to catch some, say, being realistic (9)
13 Peaceful girl past fury, one blowing top (5)
14 Literary dreamer appears in town far, far away (5,7)
18 It isn't unusual to have curries, where people can relax (7,5)
21 Overhead, a cow drops in (5)
22 Approaching a certain measure of cuisine, books entertainment venue (9)
24 Italian painter finding little to inspire his work? (7)
25 London area needing spring clean (7)
26 Far reach of wood where the enemy besieges capital (6,4)
27 No limits to perceive in relation to the listener (4)

DOWN

1 The bias about a player (8)
2 Plant is underneath wedge inscribed with mark (8)
4 Sort of nerve shown by bar assistant (5)
5 Old writer in Jerusalem, huge figure (9)
6 Is a model in an advantageous position? (7,6)
7 Name suffered when arrested (6)
8 Bell's inside with flat number (6)
10 Might gas be expected soon? (2,3,8)
15 Possible cracking of toilet pan (9)
16 Cannabis grown on the window-sill? (3,5)
17 Cryptic puzzle ultimately lush, man! (8)
19 Rodent traps doctor in shopping centre (6)
20 Monster endlessly put under pressure with order for massacre (6)
23 One's abandoned takin' chances (5)

ACROSS

1 Obsequious warrant-officer and his military force (6)
4 Fool taken in by a rugby player's left-wing hype (8)
10 Revolutionary device channelling power for the daily grind? (4-5)
11 Discourage bloke dropping off cleanser (5)
12 Pooter's sweet, but not a pushover! (7,4)
14 Triumphant cry when 23 is banished from state (3)
15 Denial from judge meeting American gangster (7)
17 Not at all negative, like Solomon (6)
19 Girl in service? (6)
21 Touching article by leader of group in shelter (7)
23 Cardinal achieved mastery in speech (3)
24 Contract a woman will put together, securing small boat (11)
26 Police officer seizing stolen garment in India (5)
27 Lacking initiative, with no time to work? (9)
29 Common soldiers given name in journal (8)
30 Write a little for small group (6)

DOWN

1 Kentish girl shown round popular college (8)
2 Stevenson, lacking a book, improvised (2,3)
3 Queen's sound accommodation for hawks (3)
5 Dress binding made by everyone in Eccles, for example (7)
6 Game merry king included among successes (11)
7 About gold missing from bridal outfit — it's turned up! (9)
8 Traveller climbing with young relative? He's the third (6)
9 Potter's craft? (6)
13 Girl's drawing producing bewilderment (11)
16 Ham, possibly, drinking in Leah's tangled story (9)
18 Traditional pen for animal features ultimately in song (8)
20 A heartless critic, one exploiting Zola, for example (7)
21 Film story about Mozart's first composition (6)
22 Bad luck some people bring? Which ones, say? (6)
25 Incident involving priest in film (5)
28 Bond's equality of attainment (3)

ACROSS

1 Vehicle that's best after testing (7)
5 Subdues a second family member (7)
9 Dance master and a star having repeated outbursts (5,4)
10 Still taking leave around end of June (5)
11 Peripheral rip in tent jerk made clumsily (3-3,7)
13 Houston regularly invested in island's oil (8)
15 Piece of cake and cream jug? Both, we hear (6)
17 Women's club about to admit British film maker (6)
19 Shark! 10 in a crowd, it's said, run (8)
22 Extraordinary brand name, good one for junk dealers (3-3-4,3)
25 Decoration I celebrate being announced (5)
26 One can be found in the Prado, sculptured (9)
27 On record as coming back down to earth (2-5)
28 Bouquet you initially get old boy to return (7)

DOWN

1 Tramp who borrows houses (4)
2 Relief troops with offensive intentions (7)
3 He's left the joint of meat for dog (5)
4 Buildings of quality (8)
5 Ratty and Mole grabbing forty winks (6)
6 Lovely Parisian who inhabits place no longer (9)
7 During practice session boy turned up and bowled over (7)
8 Alternative medicine = alternative care? Untrue! (6,4)
12 Green activist stirring up race row, one over men (3-7)
14 His last chance to play before match? (4,5)
16 Friends in short supply for so long (4-4)
18 Very important issue with rock climbing (3-4)
20 Suspended sentence? (7)
21 A cabby's moving account in superior's office? (6)
23 Beginning in October, in battle for months (5)
24 Titillating without extremely saucy clothes (4)

27

ACROSS

1 Religious leader brings a brazenness into church (6)
4 Girly heroine in little child's novel (3,5)
9 Contrary way poet writes? (7)
11 Girl's stringed instrument starts to charm audience (7)
12 Prophet introduces daughter to ceremonial meal (5)
13 Manager's dull hat (4,5)
14 First indication of guile in woman before the marriage game (5,5)
16 The missus endlessly protecting a poor child (4)
19 The PM in a big hole reportedly (4)
20 Grumble about new performer being a charity supporter? (10)
22 Aspirants for revolution? (9)
23 Perhaps Indian millions gripped by unexpected run-makers? (5)
25 Food item boy fed to goat (7)
26 Name a new ruler for Eastern city (7)
27 Retreat from hard practice having accepted proposal (8)
28 Maybe promotion of a cosmetic product (6)

DOWN

1 Bit of helmet, inch out, gives way when picked up (9)
2 Benefice reduced by a third — departs angry (5)
3 Left pencils for paints? (8)
5 Sailor's speech in Cornish location — time to go (7,6)
6 I am fish, one ultimately to do as one does? (6)
7 Persistent publicity put out by royal worker (9)
8 Impetuous driver with little yen to be crawler (5)
10 A leader with venom, a revolutionary head of state (5,2,6)
15 Avoid travel (3,6)
17 Glow of anger left — struggle to contain it (9)
18 Tricks to limit wound in place of battle (8)
21 Army seizes republic's capital (6)
22 The rod received by improper children (5)
24 State what is most important for folk to hear (5)

ACROSS

1   Thick fences top a fine old naval base (5,4)
6   Vice Chancellor with a book containing old word list (5)
9   To take a person's fish, boy you've got to be quick! (3,4,6,2)
10 Heat can make a run grim (6)
11 Corporation backing partner's held acceptable for both parties (8)
13 Stick with rugby player going through ups and downs (10)
14 Italian product needs a brief whisk (4)
16 Do like to go around start of summer recess (4)
17 In a bill, sum for arranging sort of advertisement (10)
19 To prepare for a party hire out old houses (4,2,2)
20 Composer very nearly a god (6)
23 Financial disaster to impact on West all the way (4,6,5)
24 Odd traces of giant boar one snaps in America (5)
25 Did shake obtained from milk container spill all round? (9)

DOWN

1   Character going to extremes in Sophocles (5)
2   Article transposed suggested solution in Cluedo mystery (1,5,2,7)
3   Make known girl's put on a little weight (8)
4   Liberal remains after firing whip (4)
5   Come round, in more than one sense creating alarm (4-2,4)
6   Duty on petrol, say, with third off? I'd fill the tank! (6)
7   Suffering inertia, the class daydreams (7,2,3,3)
8   Waitress suggesting cake, perhaps, hands round grand one (5,4)
12 An outburst disrupted parade ground manoeuvres (5-5)
13 Rogue that is entirely unknown to comedian (9)
15 Readily agreed to fix touring car that's overturned (8)
18 Heavenly radiator when filling a couple of pints short (6)
21 Loudspeaker turned up concealed bug (5)
22 Seize bus's occupants and steer (4)

ACROSS

1 After music, bad temper becomes sweet (6)
5 Not right to confront wickedness? Take the risk! (2,1,5)
9 Writer's block broken by girl (8)
10 Little girl, hesitate no longer capturing bishop (6)
11 Conferring, being out at elbows (8)
12 Have to take part in fixture, not one for one's country (6)
13 Revolutionary group turned back going through border (8)
15 Pretentious set of politicians lacking leader (4)
17 Plant reeds at first in wet ground (4)
19 Renounce violence where announced (8)
20 All my own work (6)
21 Caution when some energy fails in exhaustion (8)
22 Accustomed to wearing scarlet round university (6)
23 I don't know how to open beer or port (8)
24 Generous husband, to say the least (8)
25 Draw secret number — secure with it close to chest (3-3)

DOWN

2 New theorem about mass finds a measure of resistance (8)
3 Airman softly spoken, showing good manners (8)
4 Revolting, two naked old Koreans fighting (3,4,2)
5 Swimmer's courage today — fit to tour most of ocean (10,5)
6 Withdraw from activity at twenty-two (4,3)
7 Renaissance artist a bit over one's 'ead (8)
8 For instance, Bach's instrument managed to capture hearts (8)
14 Plant apple in street — one area to be avoided (9)
15 Caution — a certain food keeps only half a day (8)
16 T S Eliot receives gold trophy usually for beginners — name the poem? (2,6)
17 Measure of property for agent to shift (8)
18 Poet, right one to hold all the maps? (8)
19 Pincers for mushrooms (7)

ACROSS

1 Bond's up for being caught by the fuzz (8)
5 Prison killers caught by the fuzz (6)
9 Beautiful colour in prison boxing match (3-5)
10 Foot fault on start of boxing match (6)
12 Police so upset about terror law (4,2,6)
15 Heavenly juice from one part of apple, say (5)
16 Vowed soot should be reprocessed from room heater (4,5)
18 Dodgy meat ruins treatment against disease (9)
19 Use a disguise when talking (5)
20 They hold up light infantry men in Barchester rioting (12)
24 Open bottle — to some, exceptional risk when empty (6)
25 Plan to get rid of Christmas, one might say? (8)
26 Lead is hard to manipulate (6)
27 Approach right turning that's west of Bangor (8)

DOWN

1 Northern European soft drink is superior (4)
2 Urge to produce travel commercial (4)
3 Carnival reached by drive over quarry roads, oddly (5,4)
4 Call for dirty look when engineer enters sewer (12)
6 Honour's lost on one who's beautiful? (5)
7 A national who is about to get married in another country (10)
8 Like a nun's nursing home, with menace (10)
11 A loud traveller? One has potential to be a US citizen (4-8)
13 Ample pockets said to corrupt financial talent (5,5)
14 Hire actor to fluff line needing no response (10)
17 Space flight takes one into sun, effectively (9)
21 Grating on phone charger? (5)
22 Doormat leads to "Welcome" upon stone step (4)
23 Unknown agent rising to challenge (4)

ACROSS

1 Key a retired factory worker has left for safe-keeping (3-9)
9 The age of the bike? (5)
10 Contributor to newspaper, totally lacking in energy, composed one *Times* clue (9)
11 Breaking law, gets taken before the beak and imprisoned (6,2)
12 According to reports, Garden City is favourably situated (4,2)
13 Delinquent guys, note, can be most immature (8)
15 Fellow's aim to visit northern city endlessly put back (6)
17 Bank employee hasn't entered shillings in notebook (6)
18 Behaved amorously, being cuddled by knave, perhaps (8)
20 Where some youths might loiter like hoodies (6)
21 Having only one pound, stop going to bars in English city (2,6)
24 Complex in California, dull on the outside (9)
25 Here you are putting fuel into vehicle mostly (5)
26 Lack of interest in a point at issue (12)

DOWN

1 Structure made with expert technique (7)
2 Council's Good Pub Guide? (5,9)
3 With this I can spot rubbish! (2,3)
4 Enrolled for series of lectures, making progress as expected (2,6)
5 Report cut in incidental expenses (4)
6 Worker keeps right on supporting miners' leader (6,3)
7 Here you can get gallon, if it isn't going bust (7,7)
8 Mean crime by character that's unknown (6)
14 Insular character working in a garden (9)
16 Food makes sailor complain (4,4)
17 Game pâté for starters served in dish (3,3)
19 One's taking tablets as told after onset of debilitating illness (7)
22 Told one to quit the bar (5)
23 Writer succeeded with a succinct version of *The King and I* (4)

ACROSS

1 Awkward to do experiment involving radium (8)
5 Relative to get Old King Cole making entrance (6)
10 Rock music blaring out from auditorium every second (5)
11 Can't stop shaking, following gang: I might be jumped on (9)
12 Did like *The Times* revealing where its staff work on Thursday! (9)
13 Jobs of work with university for a feature on Morse (5)
14 Tree had pieces attached to the ground (7)
16 Colourful, neat, cutting quote recalled (6)
18 Bring small change to commercial fair (6)
20 In passing round article get two copies of *Times* (2,3,2)
22 Flower on border needs pot after time (5)
23 Attractive person should keep to the back, mind (4,5)
25 Impact golden girl makes hard to predict (3-2-4)
26 Topcoat and one end of cardigan engulfed by smoke (5)
27 S American poet, once around, has oddly to disappear (6)
28 Following shot ring the alarm (8)

DOWN

1 "We're in row three" he advises monarch (8)
2 Tiny country pub's interior managed to retain posh lifts (5)
3 Stooped, as fat person ought to, before duke (5-10)
4 Game daughter, clothing shed, looking embarrassed? (4-3)
6 Don't hold adage to be self-evident (2,7,6)
7 Order starter and eat using last of pilau, unusually (9)
8 Fellow's art deserving to be spoken of (6)
9 Nervous and upset, I retreat inside (2,4)
15 Permissive chap's got angry, apparently, on such important occasions (3-6)
17 Element supplying hotel with information (8)
19 Decapitate rat-like bats one shot with rabbit (6)
20 Sibling rivals playing tricks on royal surveyor (7)
21 Statesman put out a hand, having fended off extremists (6)
24 Dunce gets mark denoting error in dividing (5)

33

Across

1 Is careful about cutting middle joints around the mast (8)
5 Those pre-eminent in Florence really enhanced several centuries of painting (6)
9 Faculty head wanting area for study (3)
10 Party in aid of church workers (6,5)
12 God backing goddess to accept credit for Middle East incident (4,6)
13 Spring surge falls short by the start of summer (4)
15 Stumbles when entering Oxbridge's first honours exam (6)
16 Smooth coffee filling in case for flan (7)
18 Israel cunningly holding back with powerful weapons (7)
20 Victorian author's given queen an academic book (6)
23 Relative is looking haggard — that's not good (4)
24 Thin, bony girl in cover shot with us (10)
26 Plant distributing roof tiles around the Home Counties (11)
27 Sorbet's lovely with topping (3)
28 Shop permitted taking old note at first (6)
29 Robe is something worth buying for the future but not wearing (8)

Down

1 Gorgon missiles East deployed initially against America (6)
2 Participant in The Rite of Spring perhaps is rent asunder (7)
3 Craft man landed with hesitation, having policeman aboard (10)
4 Government worker upset inscrutable VP (6,7)
6 Boat service beginning on Tuesday (4)
7 Dragon dispatched, having rapier regularly plunged in (7)
8 Five hundred from Channel port go ashore — and proceed thus? (8)
11 Military dress on local with name much too high is conveying little (13)
14 Mature workers, headed by one of them — leader of team? (10)
17 Fashionable label Ultimo regularly appears — it's a gem (8)
19 Prisoner has kind wife, perhaps (7)
21 Interrupting girl with witty remark, I would be arousing strong feelings (7)
22 Particular feature of a ghost that's not concerning (6)
25 Service charge includes time and lavish entertainment (4)

ACROSS

1 Ultimately you will get commended and promoted (8)
9 Old man in charge of park — unknown fruit is grown here (8)
10 A skinflint about to produce spray (8)
11 Grouse, exhibiting low resistance to nonsense (8)
12 Drinks may be ruined (2,3,5)
14 Corruption put before a court (4)
15 In relation to transport, behave greenly (7)
17 Flower given away with note is returned (7)
21 Large sum of money producing a fraction of the optimum interest (4)
22 Novelist using girl's name (10)
23 Coming back, favourites cross the threshold (8)
25 One who chooses the Spanish or American fish (8)
26 Creature has to run away — it runs very quickly (8)
27 Contemplate miniature, one dropped and shattered (8)

DOWN

2 Game show (8)
3 Excessive light may need adjustment (8)
4 Band of regiment (horse) (4)
5 Rodents want somewhere to sleep and something to eat (7)
6 Dilapidated farm was not one of little substance (3,2,5)
7 Suitable furnishings applied to middle of home (8)
8 Place for training an official before a series of competitions (8)
13 Demotion — large one — it is staggering (10)
15 Engineers face palliative (8)
16 Hangs out with crooks and scraps (8)
18 Foreigner able to exchange a rupee? No (8)
19 Basic home man has to lease (8)
20 Ship used to dock (7)
24 Worthless group of people, 100 in all (4)

ACROSS

1   Odds against racehorse, *Royal Gem* (8)
6   Lighting-up time, one rule I'd reverse (6)
9   Carve name into piece of wood — pine (4)
10 Very ferocious, awfully loud (10)
11 People generally in near-anarchy in foreign party (10)
13 Pacific island in centre of storm bears the brunt (4)
14 A funeral song for Scotsman? (8)
16 Popular little woman arrested following bad report (6)
18 Small stones finally smaller, squashed by hammer (6)
20 Homely feature of room for army command (4,4)
22 Extra-short fight (4)
24 Huge book isn't finished, I sense (10)
26 Not agreeing to acquire saw (10)
28 Related to a head of state? That's not good (4)
29 Where traveller may keep clothes for emergency (2,4)
30 Perhaps a short acceptance of apology (3,2,3)

DOWN

2   Driver for member of upper house pockets pounds (9)
3   Austere conditions set up for us (7)
4   Standard that may be raised to no effect (5)
5   Legendary thing king pulled from stone at last (3)
6   Needs five changes to description of moat's function (9)
7   Prevent fighting — make fine beginning in force (4,3)
8   Body of water, not the first in marsh (5)
12 Conveyance to move with the waves, going to Lewis (7)
15 Relieve patriarch in a recent case (9)
17 Beneath old city in midlands kingdom, lake rapidly changing (9)
19 Part of house roofed over, and also secured (7)
21 Mean to take part in suitable aesthetic production (4,3)
23 Uncomplicated scheme I entered (5)
25 Small person said to have strength (5)
27 Commercial premises in name only (3)

ACROSS

1   Reveal opinion and beam (6)
4   Fine anger with energy released and put into practice (8)
9   Correct to get into different gear? (7)
11   Demon regarding artistic technique (7)
12   Much beside plug in electrical unit (5)
13   Fancy area in joint lacking finish and class (9)
14   Songbirds certainly not back in appealing form (10)
16   Meat in minutes eaten by dog (4)
19   Protest necessary to provide momentum (4)
20   Series of events to advertise including service ending in prayer (10)
22   Shower, getting refreshed before trendy thrash (9)
23   Discrimination, say, first taken to heart (5)
25   Set layer perhaps to insulate cold room (7)
26   Road followed by one going into eatery in city (7)
27   Lean on second artist to give someone drawing lessons (8)
28   Bug? Aid to solution gained by chance (6)

DOWN

1   Bold arbiter, expert in evil (9)
2   Soldiers led by boss beheaded member of dynasty (5)
3   Record love in a clear English story (8)
5   Benevolent proposal receives word of welcome, then matter consumes hour (13)
6   Broken maypole without a use (6)
7   Run down steps finally to board express that's turned up on time (9)
8   Top range with diamonds for crowd (5)
10   Sad song with tense words of love (5,8)
15   Figure going over the line, first person in race up a hill (9)
17   Skipper for instance bowled with quite overwhelming frequency (9)
18   Finished examination of minister's duties (8)
21   Destructive rising not long ago endlessly crushing hearts (6)
22   Drone about go-ahead nonsense (5)
24   Be quiet and get duck (5)

ACROSS

1 Review military force eating up everybody's capital (8)
5 Malevolent creature boltin' food, say (6)
8 In favour of curtailing concert (3)
9 Promotion in advance of unrest (10)
10 Booked for being uncommunicative? (8)
11 Articles in two languages about corporation's fall (6)
12 Look for Indian monotheist referred to in speech (4)
14 Sharp taste of female marsh bird? (10)
17 Disconcerted about ambassador, a shallow type (6-4)
20 In Madras, a rich garment (4)
23 Composer secures right to produce burlesque (6)
24 Painkillers? Yes and no, surprisingly (8)
25 Speeches given during summer introducing mountains (10)
26 Bath, possibly, leaving petty quarrel unfinished (3)
27 Worship always included in scripture course (6)
28 PM and art benefactor displaying sloth, for example (8)

DOWN

1 Spray from river unexpectedly mingled with soap (9)
2 Fail to keep note about agreed inspection (4-3)
3 Supreme power English politician viewed with anger (6)
4 Tease husband about present accompanying it (9)
5 Litter born in estate accommodation (7)
6 Sources of poison in workers' milk? (9)
7 One's taking maiden in so? What a neck! (7)
13 Spooner's amusing waffle, say, identifying seabird? (9)
15 What Alexander used to do for citizen soldiers? (9)
16 But surely a tramp isn't so neat and tidy! (9)
18 Cupidity, a flaw besetting a king (7)
19 Head of anemone removed from broken pea-green holder (7)
21 Rising nurse looking into a girl's memory loss (7)
22 Inventor's arrogance over broadcasting (6)

ACROSS

1 Cast having finished in audition (5)
4 Split and broken apart, in beginning (9)
9 Star performer, understanding craft (9)
10 Harsh legislator returned ring with diamond, say (5)
11 Grave situation, nothing unknown for tough girl (6)
12 Full form of meal never freely available, it's said (8)
14 Has true aim misrepresented? That's inept (10)
16 Shot relatively small number, about 50 (4)
19 Devastate in fire (4)
20 Soldier works for large-scale military exercise (10)
22 Good teacher has reason for unclear view about exam (8)
23 Keep paper together — that's the main thing (6)
26 Apart from Evelyn, nobody wrote one (5)
27 Old form of exercise helping medical treatment (9)
28 Companion the narrator had in battle on island (3,6)
29 Starts off this unusual type of reading as teacher (5)

DOWN

1 Expression of surprise seen in paintings, some painted by Gauguin (9)
2 Provide new weaponry, with specialist troops grabbing attention (5)
3 Use pedestrian method at bridge for easy win (8)
4 Number derivable from points on graph (4)
5 Nicer soups cooked in kitchen (10)
6 Prepare to publish left-wing legislation (6)
7 Representative that loudly expresses rage, initially, about party line (9)
8 Kind of clue like this, about river in flood (5)
13 Bit of Norfolk dialect for an old weapon (10)
15 Establish new sectarian organization (9)
17 European or American partners getting more serious (9)
18 Take away a couple of vehicles turning up on time (8)
21 Musician in film, starting with piano (6)
22 Polite form of address in Mothers' Union? (5)
24 Political leader isn't commonly put in the picture (5)
25 Alcoholic drink knocking out one very large group (4)

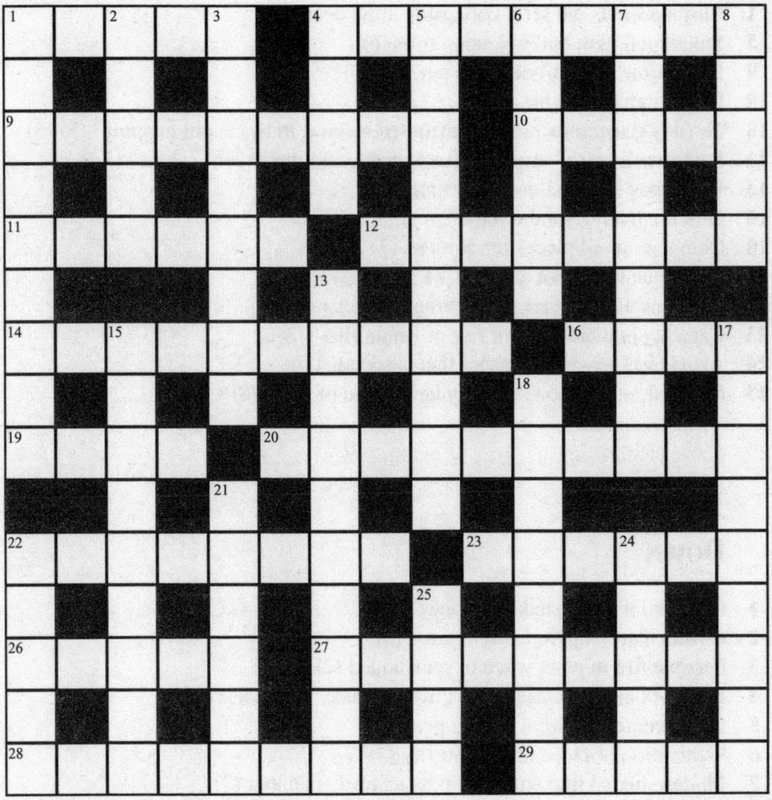
1
2
3
4
5
6
7
8
9
10
11
12
13
14
15
16
17
18
19
20
21
22
23
24
25
26
27
28
29

ACROSS

1 Most spacious old semi collapsing amid decay (8)
5 Stock food item put, say, upon rolls (6)
8 Brawl in which no-one's laid out? (4-3-3)
9 Unprofitable bank (4)
10 Terribly dangerous, when confronted by cow, to be caught napping? (5,4,5)
11 Scotsman's cry of surprise after marine creature's seen … here? (3,4)
13 What road builders do to advance (4,3)
15 Grazing land beyond river (7)
18 Compose small pieces for quintets (7)
21 Catch one who's not at home? (4,3,2,5)
22 A bit unwell, I'm perhaps lacking in energy (4)
23 Capacity one has to limit rise of Rome (10)
24 Article in French newspaper that is socialist (6)
25 See bird — cuckoo — shortly before end of April (8)

DOWN

1 Criminal ways of making money (7)
2 Covers Rover's paw, badly injured (9)
3 Terrible fire in plant when oxygen added (7)
4 In school control class — no girl may make loud noise (7)
5 Noble comrade's final resting place (9)
6 Cultivation of crops up to maturity (7)
7 Money stuffed into empty grip by a family member (7)
12 Concern to preserve distinctive feature in ornamental piece of architecture (9)
14 You'll get richer while rate fluctuates (9)
16 In which females are gripped by a strong emotion? (7)
17 One drinker beats another one up (7)
18 Qualification is framed by university official? No way (7)
19 Close to destination, we turned left in town (7)
20 Not entirely convinced about the heart of Dali being so? (7)

ACROSS

1 Sink and give up without oxygen (5)
4 Bloom is rather powdery, might you suppose? (8)
8 Team put down in more demanding region high up (9,5)
10 Most helpful report of ceremony received involving knight (5-4)
11 What comes in glory travelling around mountainous area (5)
12 Sweet musical item keeps class back (6)
14 First half of show, man, is poor (8)
17 Forbidding member of family to go outside home (8)
18 Sweet little creature protecting son (6)
20 Star in dress starts to excite luvvies (5)
22 Correct basis of conduct is needed by every individual PM (9)
24 Vehicle ran into others next to hospital worker (3,11)
25 Organise this person to follow soldier into chasm (8)
26 Man making name in country after revolution (5)

DOWN

1 Hardest areas to go round? This must be one of them! (6,6)
2 Ape needs drink, lacking energy (5)
3 Having love maybe is unprofitable (9)
4 When I had a cook round? (6)
5 Maiden cheated? That's by no means rare! (8)
6 Joint is right good place for hops (5)
7 She's large to manoeuvre, so get lifting gear (9)
9 Three schools set out a framework for home economics (7,5)
13 No burial at sea for high-ranking German (9)
15 One man's vocal quality is suitable for rock (9)
16 Gesture after race when you're desperate to cool off? (4,4)
19 County clique may have upset staff initially (6)
21 I may be after a strip club (5)
23 Keep performing somewhere in London (5)

ACROSS

1 Come across unexpectedly duff horse (4,4)

9 Loving wife's accepted kiss or messages of indebtedness (8)

10 Desert Arab perhaps converted to nudism (8)

11 Second, having finished run slowly (4,4)

12 Idiot's one rushing round moving picture perhaps (4-6)

14 It's husky: type to pull sled, ultimately (4)

15 Young birds sounding like baby seals (7)

17 Turning bend, saw dope travelling fast? (3,4)

21 Refusal to allow through small secure zone (4)

22 Operations to decrease as it were, perhaps, or close (3,3,4)

23 Sweet Nancy's an aid to Browning! (8)

25 Stride in so very loudly and leave so quietly (5,3)

26 One king in shock after another becomes reckless (8)

27 Wrong per se in backing what Wellington could have got up to (8)

DOWN

2 Standing so alone outside Queen's College, see (8)

3 Work out question, very determined (4,4)

4 Devoted sister concealing love: it's often proper (4)

5 Have more prisoners, perhaps, abandoned scene? (3-4)

6 One who's obliging can, inserting answer without doubt (3,7)

7 Study voltage to start with, before installing good fuse (8)

8 Brief items succeeded in great arenas (1-7)

13 Some reprobate atones, hating to fulfil unlikely promise (3,4,3)

15 Torn snack boxes bar empties in these bins (3,5)

16 Fine and custodial sentence after hedonistic experiences! (4-4)

18 Mum making this? Don't look! (3,1,4)

19 Scar borne by you, supporting women's reformer (8)

20 Waves at large ape, nose twitching (4,3)

24 Tiny hole said to be in bucket (4)

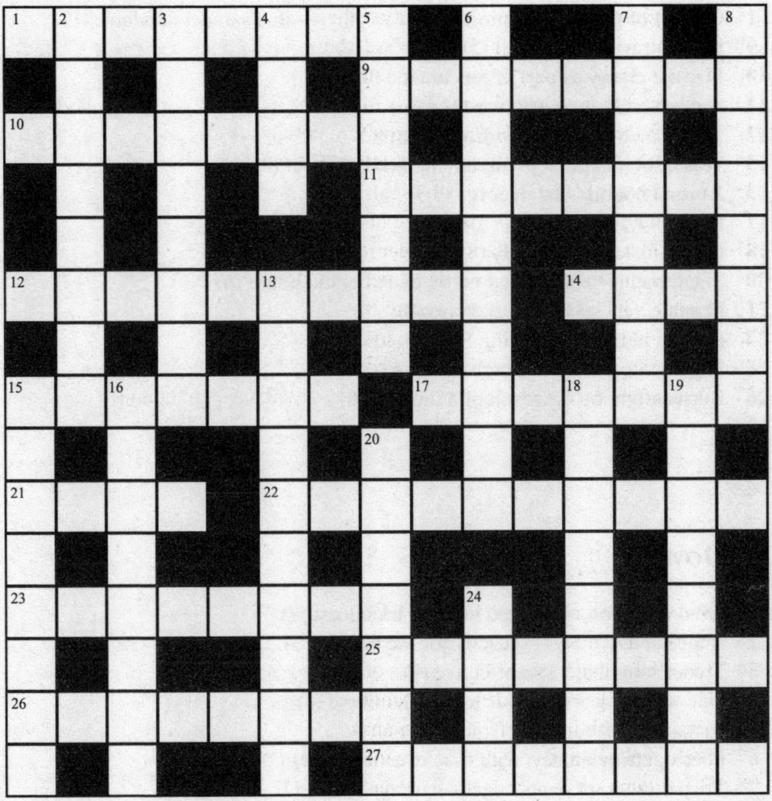

ACROSS

1 One set of good books pronounced worthy — that's understandable (12)
9 Fish — ray circling river (5)
10 Fire the clergy as part of repentance (9)
11 A good craftsman who wastes some time but gets a buzz out of his work (8)
12 The French fit into a sporting group (6)
13 Was hesitant at that point, having fiddled about (8)
15 Animal not allowed in gorge (3,3)
17 Pastry's warmer at home (6)
18 One is inside more likely (8)
20 Small meteor makes loud noise, back behind house (6)
21 Primate gets servant to exercise (8)
24 Foolish paintings showing Scottish town (9)
25 Show is for audience to see again (5)
26 Burns might be the result of a thesis (6,6)

DOWN

1 Kind of motor, note, used in radio broadcast (7)
2 Imperial assembly — strictly for the birds? (3,4,2,5)
3 Trenet song that's less effective (5)
4 One who makes demands to popular nurse (8)
5 Irritation that can hurt, from the first (4)
6 Poet's getting money, with case overturned (9)
7 Treasure-seeker pants hugely, having diseased liver (4,4,6)
8 Danger — English leaving for that reason (6)
14 Take out one man wrongly found among the most gifted (9)
16 Laid down the law if raid done improperly (8)
17 Female graduate making a complaint (6)
19 Take over from old magistrate, accepting half of lies (7)
22 European network sent up a sad song (5)
23 German produces extravagant Ring (4)

ACROSS

1 Merriment running up against duke's reserve (4)
3 One having star go with role that's fanciful? (10)
10 Notes pressure in an awkward situation to which Scott came (5,4)
11 Scottish group embracing English completely (5)
12 Brought up to swallow bait, almost made indistinct (7)
13 Oft-repeated slogan is mostly a snare (6)
15 Song Johann Strauss put before queen but not the king (8,7)
18 Shriek at one climax when involved with man (11,4)
21 What may make police investigators truthful? (6)
23 Antony's wife destroyed Cato — the Roman way (7)
26 Foreigner's a legal right to property (5)
27 I'm getting involved with no crude impropriety (9)
28 Innocent receives shocking treatment by judge in governor's office (10)
29 Public notice serious offence involving gang's leader (4)

DOWN

1 Cricketer could be lent hat? (4,6)
2 New gold rush destroys quiet for Pacific island (5)
4 A wind soon develops in this mountainous area (9)
5 Discharge man that's brought round alcohol (5)
6 What can securely fasten tress of hair on head (7)
7 Make a mistake badly in Guam, losing male soldier (9)
8 Level 21 perhaps — that's not the top (4)
9 Iranian city and country district shortly needing street map (6)
14 Support a joint game (10)
16 Highly profitable musical returns after launch oddly leads to resistance (9)
17 One way to get delivery of armour to military fraternity (4-5)
19 Unhurried pace of a new comedy writer? (7)
20 Become aware of books with fine covering (6)
22 Decoders initially crack general meaning (5)
24 Composer at a higher level displacing old, empty Donizetti (5)
25 Twist tail off crustacean that's served up (4)

ACROSS

1 Blavatsky's belief that man is in toyshop, playing (9)
6 Mean to procure empty apartment (3,2)
9 What may be worn by girl and held by boyfriend? (7)
10 Muscle providing instant power supply at the outset (7)
11 Right oven for cook (5)
12 Artist's home no longer includes shower units (9)
14 Something delightful that may quickly be stepped on (3)
15 Fortunate individual following horse for part of the way (11)
17 Polish queen, say, in neutral territory (6,5)
19 Pass as an officer (3)
20 The little pig's about last in house; wolf's second thus far (9)
22 Soldier packing grand coat (5)
24 Passion after key characters forfeited property (7)
26 Composer has baton with equipment — nought besides (7)
27 Mean street with no crossing (5)
28 Little pest making one billiard ball come to rest (3,6)

DOWN

1 Bill for losing fine drum (5)
2 Objects almost half enclosed in groups of nine (7)
3 Spot accoutrements when kings come out for pageant (9)
4 Singer opens Labour assembly (4,7)
5 You must be on time in spite of that (3)
6 Hard labour that's good and hard outside (5)
7 Musical effect and an awful lot more (7)
8 Report about Welsh river starts to save habitat for mollusc (4,5)
13 Unattractive old fur, a vile sort (3-8)
14 Beg to differ with fancy negotiator (2-7)
16 Increased rates of plain Ulster politicians (7,2)
18 Art Society — one bound to be elevated (7)
19 Bore passed by majority (7)
21 Mournful work starting and ending evensong in cathedral (5)
23 Affair one of Othello's people reported (5)
25 Moonshine over hill (3)

ACROSS

1 Composer changed bar, and put this at front of *Pinafore* (6)
4 Lowering second engine cover (8)
10 Hardy tree in trouble: don't let it dry out (9)
11 Fellow swallowing very soft fish (5)
12 Scientist's spots won't change, after star article university rejected (3,5,6)
14 Suggest feebly dropping a Liberal (5)
16 Not real coolness, entering battle: not bravery, either (9)
18 You shield criminal in unattractive fashion (9)
20 Approve of book getting smaller (5)
21 In great conflict, get back to the Earth, turning green (6,5,3)
25 Samplers of opinion bring in a native person (5)
26 January not starting pleasant: in danger of a soaking? (2,4,3)
27 Nastiest possible ogre (8)
28 Turn up wearing green (6)

DOWN

1 Is hot — strange thing for winter evening (5,5)
2 Not like hair initially in a natural cut (5)
3 Reserve army officer's fate not popular (7)
5 How confessor comes: cold and thin (5)
6 Fight — for pay rise? (4,3)
7 To work without script is accepted in one man's first show (9)
8 Hospital's appearance sound (4)
9 City copper in pile up died in the van (8)
13 No trouble on river spearing exhausted monster of the deep (3,7)
15 Stuffed extra, wearing bib (6,3)
17 Kids like us cover miles to get to resort (8)
19 Steer over Scotsman — is his cause lost? (7)
20 I must support city optimist working for gold (7)
22 Abandons treatment for eyes (5)
23 Partners shortly holding a pass up (5)
24 Leave order with computer department (4)

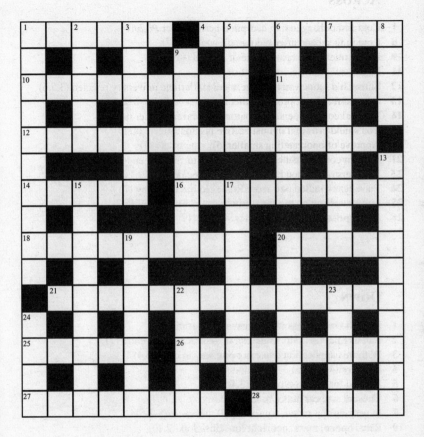

ACROSS

1 Cold and dull: monarch cancelled performance (6,2,4)
8 Cold in the shade after old flame's gone out (7)
9 Be impatient to prepare range of powers (4,3)
11 Eggs, well covered, line set of nests (7)
12 Fitting light green opening in middle of lounge? (7)
13 Lynda doing backward skipping every second gets dizzy (5)
14 Marine's leg getting strong in slow time (3,6)
16 Part of Ireland rebelled, driving away English general (9)
19 Might salesman, holding now, finally ring back? (5)
21 Duet can come unstuck as part not taken? (7)
23 You get snogged loudly — and v. red rose! (7)
24 Traveller swindled pair from Rome clothes company (7)
25 Lofty dwelling no use for stashing drug? That's life! (5-2)
26 After spillages, glumly await new soup (12)

DOWN

1 English writer cross with German's superior (7)
2 Rather like sun lamp, arguably, in skin treatment centre (7)
3 With this application one can make way in class (5,4)
4 Prisoner's here? (5)
5 Air bed for lovers, typically (3,4)
6 Unusual size car nuts (7)
7 In very upbeat mood, try some golf and cycle (5-2-5)
10 Renaissance, mark, not right for selfish folk (2,10)
15 Desire which imparts goodness (5,4)
17 Odds and ends of Victoriana you found in old jug (7)
18 Pit coal put out of sight (7)
19 Lifted up version of Bible that is wide in scope (7)
20 Important point several score (7)
22 Ultimately cagey entering as bell may sound on way out (5)

ACROSS

1   Quickly run through city with flak jacket (5)
4   Where topical messages are wrong, use sports page (9)
9   Acting profession that all kids initially enter (9)
10 Our enthralling chapters go on (5)
11 Men, exciting but backward, are wild animals (6)
12 When to knock off, roughly speaking? (8)
14 Grouse, ruff and chicken? (4,5)
16 Chaotic situation upsetting those who follow United (5)
17 Made a lot of noise, but always asleep? (5)
19 Retired idle American nurses can cut through Egypt (4,5)
21 Puzzle over second sound (8)
22 Cave's deterioration — got crumbling walls (6)
25 Spike's wrapped with string (5)
26 Administrators of university in dock see pupil's position, almost (9)
27 Horse carrying gang leader Kid Curry (5,4)
28 Form of identification plus name to access network (3,2)

DOWN

1   Surprise move for big wedding venue that overlooks Spain (4,2,9)
2   Stock car tracks (5)
3   A lot of smoke, the first sign of burning parsley for example (7)
4   In Greece, Victoria's family heading north east (4)
5   Way son is hugged by wet nurse (4,6)
6   Sentimentality fails to produce nice things (7)
7   Ocean waves advance as before (4,5)
8   Always going? Um, no toilet paper unfortunately (9,6)
13 Old hand is cut in pieces to make sliced delicacy (10)
15 A month's delay finding more central location for Royal Ballet (9)
18 Recognise one has to take risks, having succeeded in joining navy (7)
20 Sweet trolley, perhaps, a fruit's dropped on (7)
23 Good to go after weak cup of tea (5)
24 Motorsport — not a word used by occupant of tank (4)

ACROSS

1 One taking a buckshee voyage has to pack (8)
6 To speak contemptuously can cause alarm (6)
9 Go away and get busy (4,2)
10 Learned to use repetition, following lecturer's lead (8)
11 Part of record player fell to floor (4)
12 Ordered in, Roger got 23 (4,6)
14 Gold ring found in compost — that's funny (8)
16 Some phototelegraphy could be used to convey … (4)
18 … sketches in a book (4)
19 Wealth? At one point cry, being overcome, … (8)
21 … done with wealth, ruined, impoverished (4-2-4)
22 Recently getting stick out, to lash son (4)
24 Cleaner, one's mother shows attractive personality (8)
26 Caledonian jumps back in alarm (6)
27 Being overdrawn, notes in lieu of payment are repugnant (6)
28 Author's books left you taken aback (8)

DOWN

2 Subject other people to the ultimate in impertinence (5)
3 Chest of drawers could be so described — and something more (4,5,2)
4 Soak is good for nothing in battle (8)
5 Let one's work get replaced with play here (11,4)
6 Magistrate imprisons soldiers showing decrepitude (6)
7 Gentleman is retired, right? (3)
8 Real changes at uni/tech (9)
13 Talks about male amphibians (11)
15 He couldn't possibly appear in the nude (9)
17 Chamber often gets this official statement (8)
20 Secret police's period of inactivity (6)
23 Groom holding pony's head getting a kick (5)
25 A line read out in letter (3)

ACROSS

1 Use amount charged to restrict venture (8)
5 Little girl returned hit, creating commotion (6)
10 Uncertain MP soon bungled official statements (15)
11 Having enough farm accommodation, keeping a limit (7)
12 One in grass endlessly rolling over is tramp (7)
13 Free spirit? That's available drink for the audience (8)
15 Where Jacob had a dream, heading off to get woman (5)
18 Course provides connections to other websites (5)
20 Attitude taken by one lecturer, being able to create waves? (8)
23 Writer of detective books — collect about 500 (7)
25 Set to keep secret, having change of heart (7)
26 Lent's better gone somehow with smashing types carrying wine here? (3,5,7)
27 Port in dull-looking pub (6)
28 Boat's heading backwards with flighty type in control (8)

DOWN

1 Catholic offensively holy in days gone by (6)
2 An attack leads to shock military command (5,4)
3 Marks bracketing publisher's hairy bits (7)
4 Arrogant mate ending in misery (5)
6 Start off disturbance about tax being put up (7)
7 Ease off the French butter? (3,2)
8 Minutes with wrong details placed on table inappropriately (8)
9 Crosses trails running east and south (8)
14 Late performance accommodating stage character (8)
16 So, OK, whale spouts — it's a matter of scientific principle (6,3)
17 Spoilt land in part of the garden (8)
19 Warbled song the wrong way round? Must be the wine! (7)
21 One sets off ferreting — I take part, getting a lift (7)
22 Elegant girl, outwardly frigid, putting one off (6)
24 Nick's disagreement (3-2)
25 Copper piece, about eighteen inches (5)

ACROSS

1   Two books wildly amuse one foremost in Lichfield (6)
4   Hard to get into playwright, for two presidents (7)
9   Section of maths to study, tricky at heart (5)
10 Most fancy chips with last of halibut — I shall tuck in (9)
11 Fine lines at first described by bird? (5,4)
12 European visits prosperous kingdom (5)
13 Grass idiosyncratically defined: no good for grazing animals (4)
14 Food, by the way, is what scribblers live on (4,6)
18 Man takes exercise moving tree about a metre (that's several feet) (10)
20 Journey to the Western Isles, perhaps, is no end of nonsense (4)
23 War featured centrally on history course (5)
24 Railway worker is extraordinary person (9)
25 Primp around stomach, front of trousers taking precedence (9)
26 Not working so hard for papers (5)
27 Payment to traitor in residence abroad (7)
28 With help, he encumbers two men (6)

DOWN

1   In which penitent is reluctant to undergo fire and cold (9)
2   Cave churned into mud (4,3)
3   Unknown quantity announced that wretches hatefully collect (6)
4   Tiny quantity held in common (5)
5   Laughter is just the job during term (8)
6   Lab so clean, unable to reproduce results (7)
7   After the start, tie with church cut (5)
8   Erring, but one following dropped without question (2,6)
15 What may be in front of drinkers always swallowed by British with fortitude (4,4)
16 Extremely nettled, Puritan broke up game (3,3,3)
17 Tubes are briefly inserted into red wine at start of inspection (8)
19 Wrongly-defined part of horse, dad — tough! (7)
21 Periodical taker of country walks (7)
22 Words so well memorised in a film (6)
23 Pet perhaps grabs work, which may interrupt computer user (3-2)
24 Hank uses tip of needle for injection thus? (5)

50

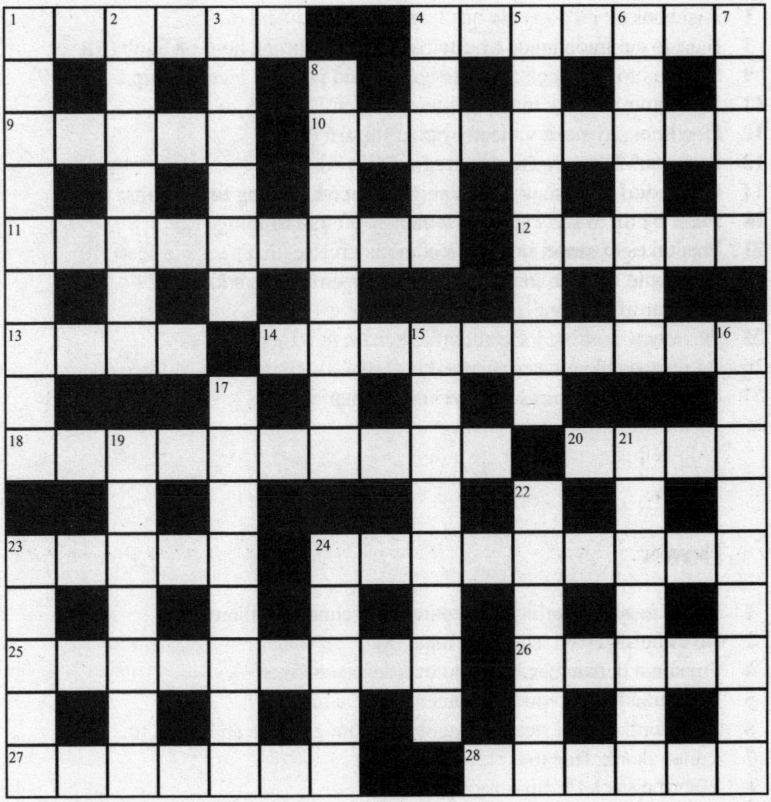

ACROSS

1 Right moan, no good (4)
3 Sign of omission made by guy perhaps consuming hour on a job (10)
9 Workers for instance carrying spades and proof of membership as well (7)
11 Delight in network reversed by irritation (7)
12 Beginning to move violently out of the ark (9)
13 Row one? That's in front part of vehicle (5)
14 Funny nod put into wordless performance following firm rhythm (8,4)
18 Plain for all to see, rabbit with energy off and running (12)
21 Presses right ahead in middle of crisis (5)
22 Academic spirit in journal apart from opening that's fantastic (9)
24 Ridicule after drone gets small rise (7)
25 Obviously nothing jolly about lieutenant in retreat (7)
26 Be responsible for a particular class (10)
27 Race ending in fracas? Matter for rumination (4)

DOWN

1 About to go into orbit, so prepared in technological area (8)
2 No more sheep on island for meat (8)
4 Tiresome person beginning to overdo sauce (5)
5 Reviser using crib possibly defended by admirer (9)
6 River with load of outstanding waterproof exercise apparatus (6,7)
7 Rotten plonk, free (6)
8 Part of speech Oedipus repeated (6)
10 Dance tune, sort played in place with low prices (8,5)
15 Critic elected to turn up and watch screening quietly (3-6)
16 Booking awful act, in for walloping (8)
17 Trusting legal document to protect river over year (4-4)
19 See supervisor in strike holding his ground (6)
20 Pro with excellence losing it late (6)
23 Sailor dismissed roughly (5)

ACROSS

1 High-class daily printed in most attractive capital (9)
6 Travel free — but there's a snag! (5)
9 Express taking soldiers into city centre, ultimately (7)
10 Astronomical phenomenon largely affecting horse and bullock (7)
11 Browning's young girl in a spot with Dad (5)
12 Cultivated swimmers are spotted here (5,4)
13 What could be a knight's fantasy, perhaps (5)
14 Ring doctor by street nearest the centre (9)
17 Thing making noise boss adapted (9)
18 Cleric caught entering through door at rear (5)
19 State university team demolished in sports meeting (9)
22 Noble of the French, withdrawing in this game (5)
24 Italian physicist taking brandy on island (7)
25 She's not a bit hard at heart (7)
26 Tropical tern featuring in children's books? (5)
27 Run over directions devised, say, for child minder (9)

DOWN

1 Charlie Parker played this live broadcast's opening work (5)
2 Poor quality sheep can get butchered at start of spring (9)
3 Woman hesitates to speak, though they take in the workers (9)
4 Current procedure for improving the railways? (15)
5 When it dawns on us that we've overindulged? (3,7,5)
6 Henry and possibly Sally's resort (5)
7 Two-wheeled vehicle carrying national leader in flowing garment (5)
8 Line Hood originally penned before noon in city (9)
13 He may have a share in cultivating the land (9)
15 Maybe 18's old message is possible to cancel (9)
16 Big box carried by odd Scottish players (9)
20 Accountant stood up and delivered bitter (5)
21 English lad skirting northern wood (5)
23 Given a hearing, remained sober (5)

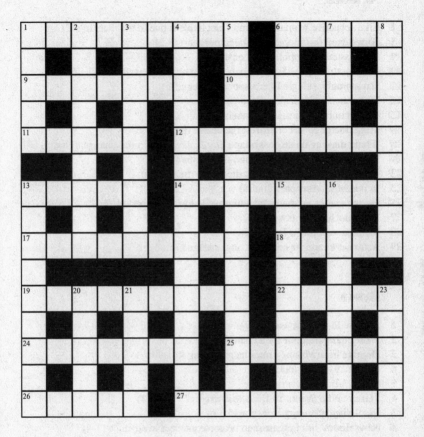

ACROSS

1 Like seductive woman, coming from bunk at five in the morning (7)
5 Tories enjoying success, as stated in report (5-2)
9 Spoil vote cast by political theorist (3)
10 Resolve to curb the French poetaster's extremes in writing style (6,5)
11 Having only a single line upset actor Ken (3-5)
12 Discover medic breaking law (6)
15 Set out to cover area such as Asia (4)
16 Magazine page has "Return of pollutant in French river" (10)
18 What editor gives those who see *The Times*, after initial change of hands (10)
19 It's not 4 but really is exquisite — the tops (4)
22 Cycling's good for one in Pacific island (6)
23 In bed, say, with spread on (8)
25 He got rounds up the spout and travelled with weapon (4,7)
27 Watering hole for lawyers (3)
28 Brogues, a dollar? (7)
29 Actor set to appear regularly on the stage (7)

DOWN

1 See a wild creature vanish (7)
2 Writer likes Rampur for a change (6,5)
3 Divulge trick Military Intelligence set up (6)
4 It's not 19 — bad luck! (4,6)
5 Fit and healthy in spring (4)
6 Seizes "Who Wants To Be A Millionaire?" prize (8)
7 I will display energy before work (3)
8 Newspapers' brief measure to promote product in advance (3-4)
13 Snack — lightly-cooked portion, under a dollar (4,7)
14 One move to get in lots of money? (4-6)
17 Poet composed sonnet about New York (8)
18 I live right in midst of trouble rising in African country (7)
20 Sign used by vendors everywhere (7)
21 Instantly in church, after a fashion (2,4)
24 Bond's enemy pursued by American intelligence (4)
26 Medic's computer file (3)

ACROSS

1 Writing in wood somewhere in Cheshire (8)
6 Initially expect Superman to need part of his costume for flight (6)
9 Runner or dramatist in play (13)
10 Ribs to order in restaurant (6)
11 A piano player's first increase in value (8)
13 Lacking a beard, was foremost in danger (10)
15 Cabbage and king (4)
16 Energy and vivacity when one's plucked Spanish flower (4)
18 Slightly amusing remark from learner in class (10)
21 Restrain worker joining strike (8)
22 Try hard run in Cornish resort, ultimately failing (6)
23 Offensively patronising prisoner being sent down? (13)
25 Way in which common man is confused by setter (6)
26 Dull leading characters in Dombey and Son — they go nowhere (4,4)

DOWN

2 One publication is associated with mass movement in poetry (7)
3 Say nothing in article probing parental intelligence (4,3,4)
4 Tongue used for thrilling osculation (5)
5 Keen to hold mug for festive drink (7)
6 Playwright's constant regret over date in Rome (9)
7 Prune found in slice of the cake (3)
8 Country girl reading (7)
12 Not at all a routine car repair (2,9)
14 Doctor finally stopping fresh rash (9)
17 Animal dancing in cabaret (7)
19 Drink four out of five brought up is made to disappear (7)
20 Sacked employee's first to leave gathering of young and old (7)
22 Topsy-turvy girl's laxative (5)
24 Niece not even born (3)

ACROSS

1 Vestment needed by some duke (6)
4 A ballet held very difficult at first — not for a beginner (8)
10 In bed, moan horribly, clutching this? (7)
11 A Catholic union concealing a mystery (7)
12 Supporter's millions rain down (4)
13 Painful period getting to place one enters, making this? (10)
15 Briefly organise binder for getting a job (9)
16 Game needs one coin, say, or another (5)
18 Spirit in the wood not sweet, notice (5)
19 Joiner in meeting-place finishing early in bad weather (6,3)
21 More plots I develop in population centre (10)
23 Light beat has power (4)
26 Done right, getting appropriate mark outside (7)
27 Lawman tucks into a chop and a drink (7)
28 Feel bad about one daughter, always in memory (8)
29 Let me show you why I say this view is unacceptable (6)

DOWN

1 In private, what every actor wants? (5)
2 Give ground — go over area of financial planning (9)
3 Submariner's warning to change direction (4)
5 One short of cash feels this drink needed (7)
6 Wren maybe giving a third off, go mad for piece of classical temple (10)
7 Poet, conspirator and wicked type, some say (5)
8 Maximum effort of ladies to secure man over time (9)
9 Leaves two at bridge to enter water (6)
14 Unable to get agreement precisely secured (10)
15 Check on walker — safe, but clutching head (9)
17 Long drink includes very soft fruit (9)
19 Peak receiving precipitation (not English) (7)
20 Prophet and priest, taking up 13 (6)
22 A possible fall of the pound sees the back of bears — bulls too (5)
24 As flower girl, rather like Daddy? (5)
25 Stick head down a bit, disfigured by this? (4)

ACROSS

1   Dig a piece of turf from the right part of Caribbean (8)
9   Some Welsh ground, I agree, turns with spin (8)
10 Earth, very fine, held in both hands (4)
11 Tailless dog, Lear character and beauty told of in nursery rhyme (4,4,4)
13 Repair to bar after receiving hard beating (6)
14 Unease with last of capital going virtually no distance! (8)
15 Place handle from lead on setter's back (7)
16 With this singer dressed for choir? (7)
20 Girl quietly hid, all worried about nudity ultimately (8)
22 Recalled perfectly fine female in love with postman (3,3)
23 Fortune obtained from a woman touring fair (1,6,5)
25 Invalid in duel, old, ignoring odds (4)
26 Some Liberals holding with fascism initially? I refuse to go there! (8)
27 Nursery gardener questioned fences I put down in the field (8)

DOWN

2   In a flash, refrain from drinking liqueur (8)
3   Dog needs rest after march with army officer (6,6)
4   Air or nitrogen inhaled by anybody running (5,3)
5   French writer pressing claim in defensive article (7)
6   Drink for one lifting medal (6)
7   US rallying champion more foolhardy when cutting corners (4)
8   Halt in city construction emptied plant (8)
12 One screwed up career in squash (9,3)
15 League champions do places for VIPs (3,5)
17 Old Irish politician turned up in Enniskillen? No, Cork (8)
18 Authoritative viewer's in possession of right answer (8)
19 West Virginian's cut bud on minute tree (3,4)
21 Eskimo conserving heat at last makes sense (6)
24 One's iced beer, perhaps, has no head (4)

ACROSS

1 On the radio get bigger hits (6)
5 In bar posh men only work so hard (4,1,3)
9 Saint leaving disguised as evil manipulator (8)
10 Address used among sovereigns — one crossing America (6)
11 Passage seen by judge during ramble around castle, say (5,5)
13 Struggle with sight (4)
14 Spice Girl entertaining Conservative leader (4)
15 Pry or sneak around being a busybody (4,6)
18 Disreputable female's list, including endless beer (4-6)
20 Main provider of awfully good exercise? (4)
21 Suit a source of joy? Not sure (4)
23 Confused doctors not nice with her (10)
25 Duck out of quarrel with a country (6)
26 Carry on or declare (8)
28 Leading journalist resisted changes (8)
29 Artist ignoring a dramatist (6)

DOWN

2 Let your hair down, as debutantes did? (4,1,4)
3 Two tricks opponents at bridge overlook (7)
4 Country with no popular spring resort (3)
5 Green stuff found in spaces between walls, say (5)
6 One using straw with drink that's an unexpected knockout (6,5)
7 Parisian who enters state positively trembling (7)
8 Couple of followers turning up, not outsiders (5)
12 Fact I point out at start of every pope's reign (11)
16 Customary scenery a TV series declined (3)
17 Charging a lot without thinking (9)
19 Touching land in a way (7)
20 Play on words about girl being a prude (7)
22 How Jersey communicated tax, we hear (5)
24 He wrote chapter to entertain mainly (5)
27 Monkey about in playgroup, mischievously (3)

ACROSS

1 Evil lunatic raves? Just the opposite (4,5)
6 Have to interrupt enjoyment in bed (5)
9 Warning from editor following line in newspaper (3,4)
10 One intervening between noble and monarch in the past (7)
11 Cause of tears, one understood by expert (5)
12 International affair put marriage under strain? (4,5)
13 Bishop, for one, that is put in power by church (5)
14 Decade of investment that was disastrous for Paris (6,3)
17 Poles asking for quick response after current's rising (9)
18 Suitably cast, finally, in adapted play (5)
19 Type of government in state I quietly despise (9)
22 Right to infiltrate fraudulent scheme to beat it (5)
24 Supposed expert on horses from one end to another? Not quite (7)
25 Car included in any financial support (7)
26 Local in Gotham? (5)
27 With which one raises a beam, about to snap (3,6)

DOWN

1 Left part of book that is very lacking, initially (5)
2 Together they rally business with clubs (2-7)
3 Without being asked, say, reworked novel? True (9)
4 As users, authors get revised reference work (6,9)
5 They must accept charge added to an account for this treatment (8,7)
6 Place to discuss ideas in class outside university (5)
7 Do a dance from the 60s (5)
8 Moving air heading towards the top of the charts (9)
13 American university's publicity included English college (9)
15 Moral philosopher, as a parent, smacked hard (4,5)
16 Drunken lot, we hear, in this drinking place (9)
20 Nobody's child left down and out? Not so, not so! (5)
21 Ruth, without husband, in short (5)
23 What's rewritten by me, including article, perhaps (5)

ACROSS

1 Wearing short pants, work for very little money (6)
4 Prevented current measure being adopted by hospital department head (8)
10 I will come in to provide standard sort of grub (11)
11 Compete no end against ace, getting through (3)
12 Evidence of clock going and stopping after losing seconds (7)
14 Herbs are great, used in regular amounts for stuffing meat (7)
15 Defiantly organised, a cleric at length's imprisoned by ghastly tyrant (14)
17 Among items on sale, easy to get horse in exchange? Not for Richard, in these (4,2,3,5)
21 Survive speaker's mocking scepticism (4,3)
22 Poet and writer held by communists in revolution (7)
23 In Europe see first appearance of migratory bird (3)
24 Speaker's right to hate ironic raving (11)
26 Daughter's given sweet sherry, sadly (8)
27 Observe husband going back into church in Lancashire, perhaps (6)

DOWN

1 Skilful feat by skier, getting boot to fit (4,4)
2 Held up first prize (3)
3 Warm drink in my mug (7)
5 Store's entire management is disorganised (3,4,3,4)
6 Model Spanish kingdom once put under pressure (7)
7 Half one country's population in crammed housing given new lease of life? (11)
8 Con and Lab fiddling expenses, initially easy to achieve (6)
9 Sailors from Plymouth left before dark in ship after storms (7,7)
13 Domestic animals linked in one sort of story one wouldn't buy? (4,3,4)
16 Alienate group of forest rangers (8)
18 Scrubber is more confident around company (7)
19 German runner's injured her shin (7)
20 Father: one's ultimate buddy? (6)
25 One bridge player holding clubs and diamonds (3)

ACROSS

1 Vera's evasion? (4-5)
6 Comes to life in holiday up north (5)
9 Bubble quietly, keeping hot, and glow (7)
10 Working dog bites head of live snake (7)
11 From area, turn back (3)
12 Crime squad at first expecting to receive boost (11)
14 Trick is dishonest, not initially attracting criticism (6)
15 Key to criminals' language — one comes out of one's shell and is taken in (8)
17 Split personality repairing raincoat (8)
19 Refuse to accept a Republican based around No. Ten (6)
22 Machine-designer's constant role changes, given more work (2,9)
23 Man's words of greeting (3)
25 Bird very cold at end of autumn (7)
27 Stole across border, one in Polixenes' kingdom (7)
28 Having run to the front, very displeased with gangly limbs (5)
29 Servant I'd found in skirmish on island (3,6)

DOWN

1 Spray water over a book (5)
2 To get into Yahoo, help arranged (4,3)
3 Almost placid North Sea rippling — it has a bobble (3-1-7)
4 Remove jumper and put off going outside (6)
5 To like the Venus de Milo is hard? It's not ugly (8)
6 Delay cancelling a clever speaker (3)
7 Fortune can be very funny (7)
8 Moving nimbly to get extra sentence overturned properly (9)
13 No all-rounder, race covered in fine sweat (4-7)
14 Weapon of unknown ability announced (9)
16 Tree makes a blaze in chimney (8)
18 Chewing action, eating cold tongue (7)
20 Not proud when deceived about me (7)
21 Head swollen in rising historian (6)
24 Questionably legal drink has no name (5)
26 See bank hasn't opened (3)

ACROSS

1 Note deposit required by one finally providing credit (6)
4 Allies set out to capture a British or Spanish queen (8)
10 Original article in outlet for pottery (9)
11 Day after Victor and Oscar initially took the pledge (5)
12 Flower arrangement regularly seen in Algeria (3)
13 A sharp spear being thrown changes one's expression (11)
14 Fisher's first from boat in Biblical city (6)
16 Surely bound to work (2,5)
19 University graduate tests first fruit (7)
20 Audible signals at side of bed disturbed sleep (6)
22 Advantageous position where car is reversed? (6,5)
25 Crow not the last companion of Pooh (3)
26 A cover said to be of use (5)
27 Wait when Ingham has left city without furniture? (3,2,4)
28 Writer, possibly, is in centre of Fleet Street (8)
29 Some pupils play in real time (6)

DOWN

1 Philosopher heard making little noise (6)
2 Frugal poet stopping penny payment (9)
3 Impose restrictions on use of moor (3,2)
5 She's eye-pleasing but out (8,6)
6 Game interrupted by female reporter in 1942 (9)
7 Letters from Sackville-West somewhere in Sussex (5)
8 Rock it and see crack (8)
9 Governor-General connected tunnels before battle (6,8)
15 After a few drinks see about a song (9)
17 Capital drug trial (5-4)
18 Gauge showing one mile covered by car (8)
21 Least successful position for weaver (6)
23 Doesn't take off underwear (5)
24 Whip revealed by characters in *Heart of Darkness* (5)

ACROSS

1   South American woman in borders of Benin (8)
5   Art work university exhibited in southern gallery (6)
10 The sort of paper whose content may make us weep! (5-4)
11 In autumn it requires a fertiliser (5)
12 Time to leave table for tea (4)
13 Slow-moving island river captured by Dutch painter (9)
15 Address to person not present that should be in St Paul's? (10)
17 Try to crash party (4)
19 Bunting seaman secured in past? (4)
20 Unexpected gen on these prehistoric pillars (10)
22 Bird that's never settled by Santa Claus? (9)
24 Bug found in new chest (4)
26 Green light taken by those on the way out (5)
27 River snake aboard extremely hot vessel (9)
28 Screen mystery (6)
29 Native American female entertaining longing to enter church (8)

DOWN

1   Resonant sound of TV equipment — it sometimes accompanies 19 (4)
2   Fire on bird crossing East Beds town (8,7)
3   Respect archdeacon bishop's left to upbraid (8)
4   Radical completely taking in a southern state (5)
6   Get on, struggling with posh language (6)
7   Another Brontë novel — not a bloke in it, naturally (2,3,6,4)
8   It polishes unknown soldiers up before pivoting manoeuvre (5,5)
9   Unidentified writer accepts advice on hard church music (8)
14 What Macavity could be, having taking ways? (3,7)
16 Dismissed Tory without qualifications (8)
18 Hazardous setting for King Edward's court (8)
21 Writer from old Republican source (6)
23 Dipper quietly leaving for lake (5)
25 Reportedly Tamworth's accommodation is an eyesore (4)

ACROSS

1   Crackers — batch mishandled by one engaged in dubious exchanges (13)
8   Proclaim loudly where musical vicar lived (4)
9   Determined, dogged girl — one after your money (4-6)
10 £1? Carpet is free! (8)
11 Sucker drops one penny in lounge (6)
13 Super daughter struggling on sort of bike — perhaps horses wanted (10)
16 Score extra (4)
17 Strong wind, but not cloudy (4)
18 Simple alert — enemy is on the move (10)
20 Margaret carrying family to capital in days of yore (6)
22 Epidemic of disease really halved in the old country (8)
24 Race, primarily for men, coming to a standstill (10)
26 Style — bootless by the sound of it (4)
27 Merchandise a girl handed in to man, a helpful fellow (4,9)

DOWN

1   I err — a tab, but it's wrong drug (11)
2   River bank robber (5)
3   One insect nailed by certain characteristic (9)
4   Take over from old official, about 51 (7)
5   Rise of young man with sex appeal that's ebbing and flowing (5)
6   Draw attention to the moon, perhaps (9)
7   21 in port (3)
12 Rapturous reception overwhelms Serb after translating comment (11)
14 Courageous action going wrong during strange rising (7-2)
15 In the middle of the street, tiny Frenchman turned up for a bribe (9)
19 Part I've got is mainly a show of conceit (7)
21 Weed in lawn (5)
23 State takes on surgeon to provide a fix (5)
25 From consultant, finally a good stock quotation (3)

ACROSS

1   Miserable place turned over by copper (3,2)
4   Emotion-inducing events? Anger fades after short time (9)
9   Plant in confined space with part of it to one side (9)
10 Country church in middle of glade (5)
11 Expected to take girl back? She may be (6)
12 Poet has broadcast live (8)
14 Partner's improvement after refreshments and pep talk? (6,4)
16 Struggle against power that's corrupt (4)
19 Come to a pre-funeral event (4)
20 Instrument for vehicle going off-road (10)
22 Player needing support after suspension (8)
23 In army group, daughter missing: taken away from parents? (2,4)
26 Traffic produces invective — one must escape it (5)
27 Significant poet I rave about (9)
28 Greeting Asian in the mountains (9)
29 Leader of Conservatives in European spin? (5)

DOWN

1   God's salutation that sends out a message of love? (6,3)
2   Numbers wanting drug, getting anxious (5)
3   Like an invention shown by office assistant in a marquee? (8)
4   Boy born … ultimate destination? (4)
5   Destroy an alien, hit at random (10)
6   A third of copper used to be hammered into money? (6)
7   I point and shout "Rover!" (9)
8   Hedge finally grows high (5)
13 Trailing under garment there's blue yarn (5,5)
15 Army chief, excellent leader of men preparing to kill enemy (6,3)
17 Exercise runs very demanding? Don't give up! (9)
18 Did warn a criminal cops might make one (4,4)
21 In election, our side were for this controversial politician (6)
22 Group about to invade spa city (5)
24 Blessed Virgin's no maiden according to heretic (5)
25 Cleric's article kept in study (4)

ACROSS

1 Good place to stand, protected from swings? (4,4)
6 Tip of finger caught in dressing fast (6)
9 Unlucky development seen in blemish: a pimple (6)
10 Preserve quiet river going into front of Edwardian square (8)
11 Often shady plant repelled new whistle-blower (4)
12 Said sailor and baker are going to sea (5-5)
14 Receiver of old devices succeeded, retaining note (8)
16 Hops cultivated and refined (4)
18 Common man embracing king: it's not serious (4)
19 Among the best is old Liberal adherent (8)
21 Height of Spain's temperature run in new order, reversed (10)
22 Character in opening of *Rio Bravo* (4)
24 Bitter words from social class after phone is cut (8)
26 Ingredient of "butter" or paste, gutted fish sent back (6)
27 Fever expected to grip England (6)
28 See Loire's sophisticated brew (5,3)

DOWN

2 Volts in an invention that's electrified (5)
3 Henna mixed with glue for intensification (11)
4 Stresses length of dash stages (8)
5 He forswore water, getting into such a state? (3,5,3,4)
6 Delicate colour of sari at first accepted by Indian (6)
7 Heed every second in Le Havre (3)
8 Decimal state, perhaps eastern European state (9)
13 Take a very soft painkiller, finally meeting resistance in narcotic (11)
15 Anger about old TV bobby turning up evidence of degradation? (4,5)
17 Exotic animal supply at dances (8)
20 Rebel supporting Anglicans in the shade (6)
23 16 in part with scum (5)
25 Upward instinctive jerk (3)

ACROSS

1 Diversions resulting from pontoon bridge splitting (4,5)
6 One water-bird on river is mature (5)
9 Child's mother holding black snake (5)
10 Firm date put out for hostile takeover (4,5)
11 Lived somewhere like Liverpool? (7)
12 Openness of university with positive attitude? Right (7)
13 Flexible in thought, in way that's enhancing (14)
17 Bad run symptomatic of what makes red cells proliferate? (9,5)
21 Person used to be seen in musical, with a piano backing (4,3)
23 Line in a great novel, unbound (2,5)
25 Hold up popular poet as one favouring wealth redistribution (5,4)
26 Seas are hidden by 'aze, reportedly, in this port (5)
27 Indicate period charm (5)
28 Writer's depression getting character on to screen (9)

DOWN

1 Squeeze some energy out of host on ship (8)
2 One responsible for capital ancient region raised (5)
3 Sporting achievement in which opponents never regain the lead (5,4)
4 Broken stones gardener put under cover (7)
5 In course taken initially, study very little (7)
6 The thinking man's sculptor (5)
7 Having nothing, under pressure, book slogger's put in? (9)
8 Kind mother, so-called (6)
14 Put together a lot of data for pub facility, perhaps (4,5)
15 Try again to meet this person's request (9)
16 Set of characters female encountered in would-be dominant church (8)
18 State of knower, confused about unknown (3,4)
19 Act like supporters in part of ground not far away (5,2)
20 Sun exposed this high-flier's mistake (6)
22 Piece of wood, a selection of which is put in box (5)
24 Page three, for example, churchman finally eliminated (5)

ACROSS

1   Supports jobs for bouncers? (9)
6   Guardian makes case for throwing out European leader (5)
9   Boat's hull (5)
10   9ed beast runs in a crazed state, wanting love (9)
11   Veteran CO is strangely at fault, engaged in military operation (2,6,7)
13   Original Pinter production in which one's appearing (8)
14   Sacred books used in distant Rajasthan (6)
16   Bird finally caught after dog's lead removed (6)
18   Men out of jail put back in chains (8)
21   Dawn chorus (5,3,7)
23   Kid at home organised musical entertainment (3,6)
25   Heard farm labourer's hymn (5)
26   Expression of disgust about part of Canada (5)
27   Teacher faces resistance by class in northern town (9)

DOWN

1   Music is constant during party (5)
2   Old theatre company upset about getting rid of diva (5,6)
3   Sickly-looking child needed coat (7)
4   Aussie PM briefly embroiled in scam is certainly not scoffing (8)
5   Snack: double portion of it served with instant filling (6)
6   Round end of plain, road bends right, leading to a mountainous region (7)
7   Stump up for some shock treatment (3)
8   In the main I'm seen as rock singer (5,4)
12   Clever chap appearing at end of popular TV broadcast (11)
13   By and by begrudge going into work (9)
15   Mad clown performing still (4,4)
17   See Welsh woman at bottom of some fields (7)
19   Roman general's command accepted by a governor (7)
20   Home help available (2,4)
22   Groan heard, oddly, from him? (5)
24   Rating queen higher than king (3)

67

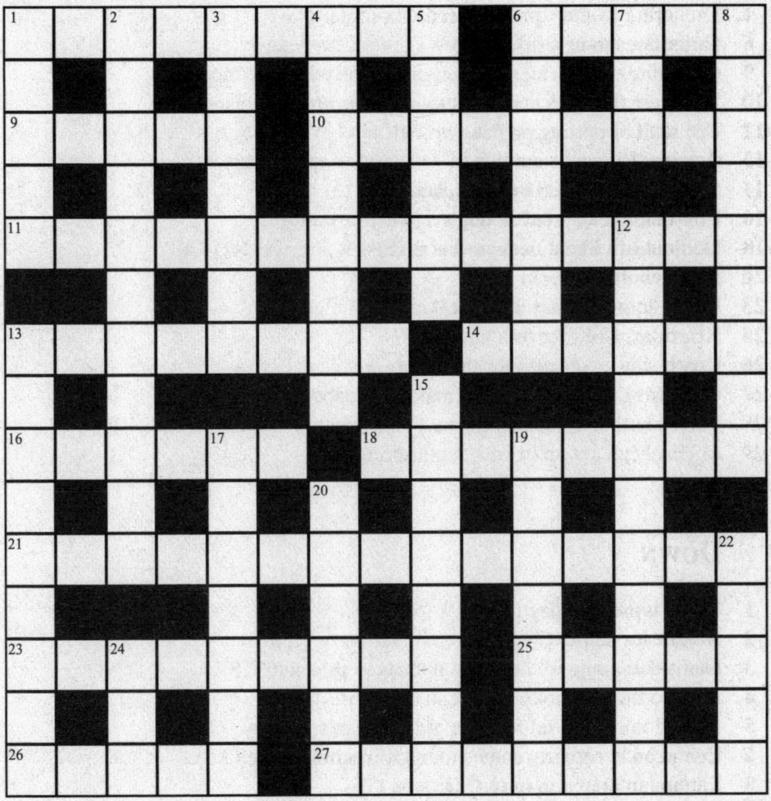

ACROSS

1   Excluding women, project needs six-footer (4,6)
6   Sailor goes to new lake (4)
9   Get along with former partner, one involved in sacrifice (2-5)
10 Troublemaker gets head of Russian government replaced (7)
12 The skill of putting on *Pinafore*? (10)
13 A point that's relevant (3)
15 Clods are disturbed by this school (6)
16 Column, one covered in rendering (8)
18 Oddly, team like quiet at work: discuss it afterwards? (4,4)
20 Join new driver in car (6)
23 Vessel in stream not British (3)
24 After veg, a boy leaves (5,5)
26 Credit, say, is secured for the oven (7)
27 Collapsing pound — it's the national symbol (7)
28 Make another version of poem, beginning to read from the back (4)
29 Michael can get upset without thinking (10)

DOWN

1   White wine is in bag (4)
2   A superior helper (7)
3   Game that's big, we hear, but it leads to prison (6,2,5)
4   Referee finally books reserve in draw (6)
5   Record taxi's arrival for start of President's journey? (3,5)
7   European eventually comes round, if nothing more (2,5)
8   Entrant so prepared to run? He won't (3-7)
11 Optional arrangement to support further inference (13)
14 He has weight to shift — try joining club (4-6)
17 Very lazy slob, one I'd let take part (4,4)
19 Gun one lad let off without enthusiasm (7)
21 Finally gets into film, using credit card (7)
22 Grab and beat up in school (6)
25 River fish: start to land it? (4)

This was the first qualifying puzzle for the 2009 Times Crossword Championship.

ACROSS

1 From rebound, defender to shoot (8)
5 Compensate for cancelled series (6)
10 Victor heading off in private (5)
11 Left wearing more unusual choker (9)
12 Vessel, monster, short of fuel (9)
13 Groups hold clubs in schools (5)
14 Late extra expected (7)
16 Obtain drug, legalised (6)
18 Female in hat stripped (6)
20 Mother drawing spy in colour (7)
22 Giant butterfly (5)
23 What may be wheeled in spa, daily around one? (4,5)
25 Ambassador's enthralled by sign in reference book (9)
26 Old unaltered haven (5)
27 Spit in bar in Germany (6)
28 Revealing lines suppressed by Attlee, deviously (8)

DOWN

1 Book trendy resort (8)
2 Defeated a northern European, breaking record (5)
3 Really, there must be nutrients in desert (3,8,4)
4 Faggot, using last of liver, is one (7)
6 Girls' college going through the whole of coach (9,6)
7 Pick leader in secret ballot (9)
8 Push one's way through American street (6)
9 Screen restaurant, English (6)
15 Ivy, perhaps, always growing (9)
17 A pass splitting the French in game (8)
19 Thanks poet in a jerkin (6)
20 Painter, as *Times* broadcast (7)
21 Mother embracing son — what might he be called? (6)
24 Confused sailors often are (2,3)

This was the second qualifying puzzle for the 2009 Times Crossword Championship.

ACROSS

1 Begin to understand, getting on with this material (6)
4 Indicter rejects bill, enthralling male shopper (8)
10 Silent about woman beginning to install element (9)
11 Restriction relating to fat cat (5)
12 Sweet basil, say, planted outside? (7)
13 Cipher: an obsession with a small number (7)
14 Woman char carrying large vessel (5)
15 Toast a couple of mates left unfinished (4-4)
18 Instrument fellow 13 returned after party (8)
20 Surprised expression of Scot dipping into mother's coffee (5)
23 Licensed trade may be decentralised as such (7)
25 Attack doctor dividing committee (7)
26 Part of Asia Minor once featuring in scholarly dialogue (5)
27 Clumsy gal in teens dropping spades when disturbed (9)
28 Blow up daughter, rejecting any child (8)
29 Like 2's journey into outskirts of Shrewsbury (6)

DOWN

1 In church, a member's appeal for holiday accommodation (4-4)
2 Fierce woman inserting single key in lock (7)
3 Where enthusiasts go without getting wet? (9)
5 Slips, possibly, that may never be alluded to! (14)
6 Land must ultimately occupy a position in it (5)
7 Cocktail in Paris that's lacking in a Caribbean island (7)
8 Go back, for example, given Frenchman's protection (6)
9 Not the first press writer to be an infiltrator! (5,9)
16 Dairy product honoured writer placed in horse-drawn vehicle? (9)
17 Gangsterism is too rife at first in trade (8)
19 A group, working, give up (7)
21 Hotel group briefly keeping a little butter for bread (7)
22 Party over, youth delivers sentimental song (6)
24 Papers covering lecturer's initial field of study (5)

This was the third qualifying puzzle for the 2009 Times Crossword Championship.

ACROSS

1 Somehow from capitalism you'll get what oppressed people may need (9,6)
9 Significant events in German area with its money gone (9)
10 Gas from old vessel added to nitrogen (5)
11 Vehicle is hard to move out of sight (6)
12 Sailor prophet's holding at a distance (8)
13 Standard series of actions you announced in sham trial (6)
15 Local supporter doesn't allow person to be exploited (3,5)
18 Responded from all directions, interrupting a Socialist (8)
19 Manoeuvre to perform in movement out of control (6)
21 Mouth has little point, when one's restricted as this? (8)
23 African songbird, it's claimed by us (6)
26 Pick selection from comparative literature (5)
27 This redundancy could mean an awful lot to a guy (9)
28 Whereby people, by turns, get elevated or brought down (6,9)

DOWN

1 State supporting China in extended discussion (7)
2 Material that's given blanket coverage (5)
3 Daily rush to achieve some accommodation (9)
4 Either end of composition is banal material (4)
5 Girl embracing star in entertainment capital (3,5)
6 On which notes are written for teachers (5)
7 Drunken yob monarch left in prison inmate rejected (5,4)
8 Marine trained on lake that's salt, for one (7)
14 Maestro of Italian opera, having popularity rising repeatedly (9)
16 Players come and go here, providing opening for coach (5,4)
17 Modern sources of information Fabian quotes soundly (8)
18 Like Eliza, initially, or 'Enry 'Iggins, say (7)
20 Political historian getting Conservative really mad (7)
22 Work religiously done as equivalent of PE? (5)
24 Instrument woman played like a man (5)
25 Ursa Minor observed on a tropical island (4)

This was the fourth and last qualifying puzzle for the 2009 Times Crossword Championship.

ACROSS

1   Rabble in troubled isle die to get out of action (10)
6   Sell very last part (4)
10   Bachelor introduced to a south-eastern European who's coordinated and flexible (7)
11   Moronic, bumbling character from Aristophanes (7)
12   Puncher shackling deviant is the one with kinky tastes (9)
13   Ingredient in healthy meals? (5)
14   Poet and librettist united in a low place (5)
15   Partner, once saintly, seizing gun to clean up (9)
17   Successful shopper's expression of contentment about hunt (9)
20   Line in verse starts runs (5)
21   Runs in a line that indicates direction (5)
23   Ultimately, Marcel Marceau enters to marry lover in pantomime (9)
25   Tuck in such shiny sheets? (7)
26   Fast talking person who teases (7)
27   Perhaps referring to Guy's with health problems (4)
28   A veil may be drawn over this pile of literature (10)

DOWN

1   Tower over heart of Mordor's fighting Frodo at the outset (5)
2   English Queen hurt those without commission, introducing raised tax (4,5)
3   Stranger with beans, booed for panto? (5,2,3,4)
4   Coffee with foam involves one topping of cinnamon grating (7)
5   Quickly get high and scare away sheep (5,2)
7   See about a fifth of interest in advance (5)
8   Sand ridges covering general southern shingly headland (9)
9   See me win icy sport, curling across lake, here? (6,8)
14   One who prepares the way, a description of St Patrick? (9)
16   I've received a post: copy's content is endlessly incisive (9)
18   Cryptic clues are nearly profane (7)
19   Described as family (7)
22   Raise as standard approach (3-2)
24   Top royal flush's colour was mistaken (5)

This puzzle, used in the First Preliminary round of the 2009 Times Crossword Championship, was solved correctly within the time limit by 68% of the competitors.

ACROSS

1 Rough patch as brain is muddled without oxygen (8)
5 Make slow progress on son's bad handwriting (6)
10 Wild allegations are adding in pressure that keeps partners apart (5,10)
11 One holding hands with me to cross tricky canal (7)
12 Core group of students around London college taking Ecstasy (7)
13 Unfinished short story about office worker's scorn (8)
15 Line leading beast of burden round? (5)
18 Incessant talker's not good as a court official (5)
20 Number by Chopin, primarily — an artist coming to a premature end (8)
23 Doctor Who … at all times, at all events (7)
25 Tearfully sentimental girl wants nothing in return (7)
26 Concealed detector for articles moving from Paris to London via Berlin? (5,3,7)
27 Gallery worker's rage following opening in Hayward (6)
28 One new disc includes track that's tipped (8)

DOWN

1 Coolness of a place above burial vault where temperature's dropped (6)
2 Managed to tease about rising significance of green curry (5,4)
3 Petition that's very much allowed by the courts (7)
4 Being this, fitting into robes execrably? (5)
6 Part of church fortune lost with departing old saint (7)
7 A tree's lost its top, but certainly not dead (5)
8 Wishes to get best position on the field (8)
9 Very attractive and enchanting quality about fine fabric (8)
14 My French chief last to fly, a casualty of the Revolution (8)
16 What bridge player might lead twice to give information away (9)
17 What's being treated as "Ssh"? Uh-huh! (4-4)
19 Mental abstraction constantly occurs in the midst of grief (7)
21 Exceptional university learner is after gold star when going up (7)
22 Home and money reportedly possessed since birth (6)
24 Open up dive in Mayfair? (5)
25 Half a day drinking appellation contrôlée burgundy (5)

This puzzle, used in the First Preliminary round of the 2009 Times Crossword Championship, was solved correctly within the time limit by 70% of the competitors.

ACROSS

1   A reflective detector, in two senses (5)
4   Passed away, keeping calm and refined (9)
9   Riding, can put in an order here? (6,3)
10 Italian saint is taken off coin (5)
11 Powerful person rolling in — see me cringe (8,5)
14 Something heavy? Boy should carry nothing (4)
15 Person outside a Cambridge college with a chemical for cleaning (6,4)
18 She's chipper at her work (10)
19 With'old a suggestion for action (4)
21 Bill may have this extra career backing church activity (7,6)
24 Some bile accumulating in part of the gut (5)
25 Girl's pleasant, not one for irritability (9)
27 Maybe train official men after short prayer (9)
28 Painter who returns two hours before noon (5)

DOWN

1   Beginning to rampage like a bull (but not a cow!) out of control (10)
2   Academic celebration never ever to be forgotten (3)
3   Team's guest player gets double (6)
4   Something awkward to put up? Spooner's to monitor challenge (4,5)
5   Child succeeded on TV show maybe (5)
6   Break during festival at Edinburgh? (8)
7   Pleased, in one interpretation, to be tenant (11)
8   One's needed to break it in (4)
12 Hazel's home, very succinctly described (2,1,8)
13 Administration of capricious magnate restricting chaps (10)
16 Police officer of power in home territory (9)
17 Vehicle flipped over in heap after opening of sunroof for somewhere to breathe (8)
20 Warrant officer, about 23, expresses desire for peace (6)
22 Contribution of one penny accepted by head (5)
23 Potential riser in the charts — or potential slipper? (4)
26 Greek character with name for being religious (3)

This puzzle, used in the First Preliminary round of the 2009 Times Crossword Championship, was solved correctly within the time limit by 61% of the competitors.

ACROSS

1 Group given useless information at first (5)
4 Carrying class on outing, coach goes round place in Soho perhaps (5,4)
9 Bright signal of hardly any significance? (4,5)
10 Idle, I had left after head count, for one (5)
11 Female production of *Hamlet* (6)
12 Lady bringing fortune, Spooner said, for a loser (4,4)
14 Each can have taste of Paris, dining chez Maxim's? (6,3)
16 Plant in Morecambe area (5)
17 Lots of publicity surrounding American president (5)
19 Send off a packet at last, enclosing very popular copy (9)
21 Former wife minded being stretched (8)
22 Food given to son making him regular (6)
25 Certainly no better who's risked the odds (5)
26 Enjoying salsa, perhaps, eating very early (2,7)
27 You take lead off pets and you can bet they'll run (9)
28 Good fellow put back toilet seat (5)

DOWN

1 Let slip drop too many vital catches? (4,3,4,4)
2 Be inquisitive about origin of Romance language (5)
3 Grundy unattended on day he was born (7)
4 Drop article that's long and rambling? (4)
5 Withdrawal of soldiers needing treatment for broken bones (10)
6 Trouble seeing monkey half-hidden in tree (4-3)
7 Liberal concerned to secure pay increase shortly as workers' champion (9)
8 Supply unlimited bran flakes, and create this? (9,6)
13 Motorway police not terribly close (10)
15 Top-class crumble and pie served up in restaurant (9)
18 Notice lake's stocked with fish (4,3)
20 Notes questionable vote as Conservative gets in (7)
23 Prevent Anna abandoning piano for another instrument (5)
24 Fish battered and subsequently served for starters (4)

This puzzle, used in the Second Preliminary round of the 2009 Times Crossword Championship, was solved correctly within the time limit by 63% of the competitors.

ACROSS

1   Secure load carried over the hill heading west (7)
5   Incense queen during spell without power (7)
9   Where cruise passenger is to cut cards twice? (11)
10 Obnoxious fellow stood, having to leave (3)
11 Made English composer finish off record (6)
12 Name prey taken out of the sky (8)
14 Penitent woman confusing medley with anagram? (4,9)
17 Captain wasted sailors, as best managers may do (3,1,5,4)
21 Low charge way to get lots of bits of music? (8)
23 Take out article to boil (6)
25 Turning round, hold up stick (3)
26 Force secret out of wife, a successful competitor (11)
27 Light spin finally used in delayed service (7)
28 Posh look in extremely trendy Italian region (7)

DOWN

1   Game of mine stopped by what in Spain? (6)
2   Cutting remark about a farm animal's picture (7)
3   Continually busy time after moving to North East (2,3,4)
4   Edge of the stockbroker belt (4)
5   All too powerful male just executed, in past year (10)
6   He leaves the very good sweet wine (5)
7   Gold trees waving in plain (7)
8   Compromise and calm down (8)
13 European fighter helping resettlement (10)
15 Events in the field making his cattle go to the dogs? (9)
16 Big-spending friend holding party turned up in costume (8)
18 Journalist beginning to see through Cardinal (7)
19 Plant is special one girl potted (7)
20 What upset bohemian is rude (6)
22 Drinks announced for interval (5)
24 Closest times seen during final (4)

This puzzle, used in the Second Preliminary round of the 2009 Times Crossword Championship, was solved correctly within the time limit by 51% of the competitors.

ACROSS

1 Bend, then hit dog (3-3)
4 Map indication is different, then miles behind (8)
10 A stag party firstly seeking vocalist (9)
11 Light cutter in sea tossed from side to side (5)
12 While quiet, one's deadly (3)
13 In the cooler, crack military leader, an armed chap (11)
14 Post reaching London area far from plentiful (6)
16 Where directors are all at sea, perhaps? (2,5)
19 Vehicle with a nearly peaceful cat (7)
20 In lead, decision-maker requiring a construction that's simple (6)
22 Pictures horse captured by caveman, rope finally in a hoop round the legs (11)
25 Growth after forest fire? (3)
26 Animal with fur is commonly less cold (5)
27 Rock covers a failure, missing on radio transmitter (9)
28 Boy turns to start to sing, say, number from where marked in score (3,5)
29 Lie, say, getting to floor (6)

DOWN

1 Prowler died, caught in embrace of creature of the night (6)
2 With everyone beginning to panic, then gorilla runs — it's a stick-up! (9)
3 Asian turning up any time now? (5)
5 Forger's plant is busted — one hangs by the neck (6,2,6)
6 Foreign article exposed group's uprising as fair (9)
7 Rider given order to support English racing here (5)
8 Pickle created without a bit of bacon, unfinished (8)
9 Old cook protects underside of loaf rising in dish (4,10)
15 People with covering for legs saving rupees for jumper, say (9)
17 Sculptor's material, a bloomer being experimented on? (9)
18 Turpin's last mount's gone over in burn (8)
21 Exhibit emotion hugging that woman, one with a heart of stone (6)
23 Mammal separately packaged (5)
24 Measure police required, six-footer (5)

This puzzle, used in the Second Preliminary round of the 2009 Times Crossword Championship, was solved correctly within the time limit by 48% of the competitors.

ACROSS

1   Fall for visitor (7)
5   Business with element of rock and roll ultimately ridiculous (7)
9   Let rip and boo terribly inferior work (9)
10 Lament loss of second container (5)
11 Parasite regularly depleted blood, unseen (5)
12 Suddenly almost splitting open (9)
13 Is sanction one to disrupt present objective? (13)
17 Baron perhaps broke apart from bishop and king in country with agenda? (13)
21 Opt for refined fuel, on reflection, in range of investments (9)
24 Following drink with consumption of second is wrong (5)
25 Wearing, undesirable experience (5)
26 Raced around field, catching horse in lead (9)
27 Rule that is not just unknown in radio (7)
28 Neutral annoyed to be involved (7)

DOWN

1   Raise pressure to cut tricky stock (6)
2   Inaccurate and used to being knocked for six (9)
3   Paradise, first off, inhabited by a certain female with pride? (7)
4   Feel elated, having small part in play broadcast (4,2,3)
5   Caution required to guard against cut (5)
6   People having paid nothing about to get reminder (7)
7   Unspecified number in haul, caught earlier, stuck (5)
8   Stage of journey covering north before next stretch (8)
14 Drama that goes on to increase with church leader's intervention over article (4,5)
15 Major route blocked by hostile troops (9)
16 Locate work and hurry up with suggestion, not hard (8)
18 Flavouring initially somewhat slight, lacking finish (7)
19 Hellish area? Gather far from it (7)
20 Hawk in ascent from field depicted (6)
22 Competitor right at top of tree (5)
23 Strong heart of populist rising above filthy place (5)

This puzzle, used in the Grand Final of the 2009 Times Crossword Championship, was solved correctly within the time limit by 22 of the 24 competitors.

ACROSS

1 Gas mark is reset for peckish errand boy? (9)
6 Finally sails boat via Calf of Man (5)
9 Man carries round fish for the bulk of the population (7)
10 Not at ease with small hugs (7)
11 Fluff from last of wool leaving unsightly mark (5)
12 Bats flying as standard here (2,3,4)
13 Island where sea is warm and air is fresh (8)
14 Composer's Mass, largely obscure, that could be hit (4)
17 Chauffeur to be flash, possessing one? (4)
18 Garment in which to clear quarterdeck (8)
21 Pack of fish appropriate burden for student? (9)
22 House accommodating parties and raves about to get a mention (5)
24 Town that's deserted on a Thursday (7)
25 Busy training: time flies (7)
26 Finished grand fitting round bend in pipe (5)
27 State angel's regularly in perhaps perfect ecstasy (9)

DOWN

1 Odd bits of boat break going round spit (5)
2 This photo of her married is grotesque, to be frank (5,4,3,3)
3 Leggy creature with a bust seen outside church before noon (8)
4 Puritan's unnatural influence on old empress (8)
5 Change some ingredients to get a tummy upset (6)
6 Activity centre commandeered by Sister for Quaker movement (6)
7 Trainee pilots miss home, perhaps like hand-to-hand fighting (2,5,8)
8 Something done up in bags? Import's one that's boxed (9)
13 Pitch area, not so short, encircled by track (5,4)
15 Daughter stopping profit from firearms becomes poetic hero (5,3)
16 Ideal arrangement, except in retirement (5-3)
19 What violinist gets when preparing to leave stage (3,3)
20 Sailor on plane circling about base (6)
23 Humble English cod is superior! (5)

This puzzle, used in the Grand Final of the 2009 Times Crossword Championship, was solved correctly within the time limit by 11 of the 24 competitors.

ACROSS

1   Does "cheer" mean this? (7)
5   Burn bridges in part of grand Scottish city (7)
9   Bugs in Vista when installing game software (9)
10 Remove starter of old seafood (5)
11 Neighbour of Iraq is finally open to the West (5)
12 Ball lifted accurately in golf — ideal shot (5,4)
14 Bomber making you keep up? (6,8)
17 One trying issue of *Paris Match*? (6,8)
21 To increase nursing one that does extra duty (9)
23 Several wives are preferred to one for him (5)
24 Flag day's opening turned bad (5)
25 The volume one chooses for listening? (5,4)
26 Field dressing put to cut (7)
27 Bats eyelid — diamonds given (7)

DOWN

1   Rider has reason to keep left (6)
2   Virgin heads for nunnery across the river (7)
3   Head off flight after ex-pupil's removal (9)
4   Four jockeys among crew on Monarch aircraft (11)
5   Laugh — short convulsive breath (3)
6   A completely empty bypass (5)
7   Yellow Submarine's finale? Mouth organ coming up (7)
8   Device to carry on ship? (8)
13 Green celery — find nothing amiss (3-8)
15 From part of leg, short thin sort of pencil lines gone (9)
16 Defuses bombs? Pressure told (6,2)
18 Always leave and manage to return (3,4)
19 Chap restricting runs with balls? (7)
20 Had a bad habit cured (6)
22 Animal house has one very quietly feeding (5)
25 Pose in Sun, topless (3)

This puzzle, used in the Grand Final of the 2009 Times Crossword Championship, was solved correctly within the time limit by 17 of the 24 competitors.

1

2

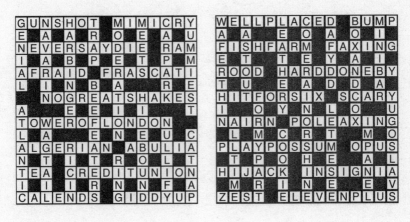

3

4

SOLUTIONS

5

6

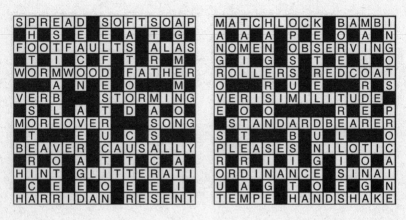

7

8

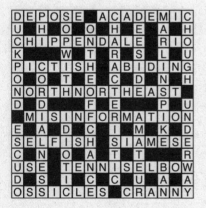

9 **10**

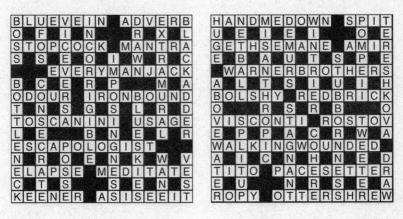

11 **12**

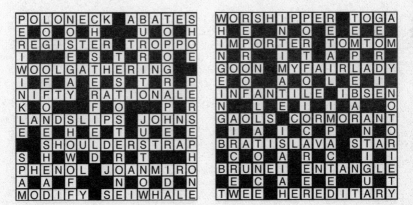

SOLUTIONS

13

14

15

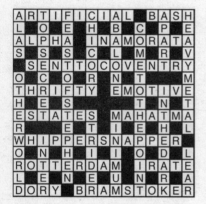

16

17

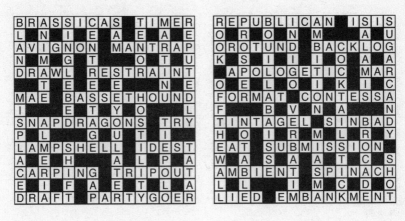

```
B R A S S I C A S   T I M E R
L   N   I   E   A   E   A   E
L A V I G N O N   M A N T R A P
N   M   G   T     O   T   U
D R A W L   R E S T R A I N T
    T   E   E   E     N   E
M A E   B A S S E T H O U N D
I   E   E   T   Y   O     L
S N A P D R A G O N S   T R Y
P   L   L   G   U   T   I
L A M P S H E L L   I D E S T
A   E   H   A   L   P     A
C A R P I N G   T R I P O U T
E   I   F   A   E   T   L   A
D R A F T   P A R T Y G O E R
```

18

```
R E P U B L I C A N   I S I S
O   R   O   N   M     A   U
O R O T U N D   B A C K L O G
K   S   I   I   O   A   A
  A P O L O G E T I C   M A R
O   E   L   O   I   K   I   C
F O R M A T   C O N T E S S A
F   B   V   N   A       N
T I N T A G E L   S I N B A D
H   O   I   R   M   L   R   Y
E A T   S U B M I S S I O N
W   A   S   A   A   T   C   S
A M B I E N T   S P I N A C H
L   L   I   M   C   D   O
L I E D   E M B A N K M E N T
```

19

```
S A G A   S C H O O L M A T E
  M   U   C   A   T   U   Y
R O T T W E I L E R   O D E R
  N   H   P   L   A   I   I
U T M O S T   O M N I V O R E
  I   R   I   F   T   E
A L O E   C A R T O O N I S T
  L   S   E   O   O   U
M A R S H A L S E A   C A S T
  D   N   I   L   T   C
B O N D M A I D   A N U B I S
O   I   T   E   R   R   T
G O T H   O R N A M E N T A L
U   R   M   C   E   A   T
S L E E P Y H E A D   L E E K
```

20

```
K A N G A R O O J U S T I C E
I   O   F   R   A   I   N   X
L E T H A R G I C   B A C U P
L   E   S   Y   O   Y   O   O
J U D I T H   A B A L O N E S
O   B     I   C   E
Y U M Y U M   S T J A M E S S
  A   C   M   E   D   R
F O R T K N O X   G U S T A V
I   I   N       L   E
B E J A B E R S   S T A G E R
R   U   R   O   O   E   A   O
O R A T E   V E S T R Y M A N
I   N   D   I   L   E   M   A
D E A D A S A D O O R N A I L
```

21

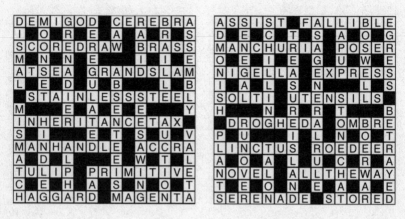

```
D E M I G O D ■ C E R E B R A
I ■ O ■ R ■ E ■ A ■ A ■ R ■ S
S C O R E D R A W ■ B R A S S
M ■ N ■ N ■ E ■ I ■ I ■ E ■ ■
A T S E A ■ G R A N D S L A M
L ■ E ■ D ■ U ■ B ■ ■ ■ L ■ B
■ S T A I N L E S S S T E E L
M ■ ■ E ■ A ■ E ■ E ■ ■ ■ ■ Y
I N H E R I T A N C E T A X ■
S ■ I ■ ■ E ■ T ■ S ■ U ■ V ■
M A N H A N D L E ■ A C C R A
A ■ D ■ L ■ ■ ■ E ■ W ■ T ■ L
T U L I P ■ P R I M I T I V E
C ■ E ■ H ■ A ■ S ■ N ■ O ■ T
H A G G A R D ■ M A G E N T A
```

22

```
A S S I S T ■ F A L L I B L E
D ■ E ■ C ■ T ■ S ■ A ■ O ■ G
M A N C H U R I A ■ P O S E R
O ■ E ■ I ■ E ■ G ■ U ■ W ■ E
N I G E L L A ■ E X P R E S S
I ■ A ■ L ■ S ■ N ■ ■ L ■ S ■
S O L T I ■ U T E N S I L S ■
H ■ ■ N ■ R ■ R ■ ■ T ■ ■ B ■
■ D R O G H E D A ■ O M B R E
P ■ U ■ I ■ L ■ N ■ O ■ T ■ ■
L I N C T U S ■ R O E D E E R
A ■ O ■ A ■ L ■ U ■ C ■ R ■ A
N O V E L ■ A L L T H E W A Y
T ■ E ■ O ■ N ■ E ■ A ■ A ■ E
S E R E N A D E ■ S T O R E D
```

23

```
S T R E T C H E R ■ H A Z E L
I ■ E ■ O ■ E ■ E ■ A ■ I ■ O
G L A S S ■ D I P S W I T C H
M ■ D ■ C ■ G ■ A ■ O ■ ■ ■ E
A N I M A T E D C A R T O O N
N ■ ■ L ■ R ■ K ■ T ■ F ■ G ■
H U G U E N O T ■ C H A F E R
O ■ G ■ ■ W ■ L ■ ■ ■ I ■ I ■
L E A N T O ■ P E M M I C A N
D ■ O ■ I ■ A ■ G ■ A ■ E ■ ■
W E L L E S T A B L I S H E D
A ■ ■ D ■ R ■ R ■ D ■ O ■ A ■
T R I L O B I T E ■ I E U A N
E ■ M ■ W ■ U ■ A ■ S ■ R ■ C
R I P E N ■ M A K E H A S T E
```

24

```
T I C K ■ H O R S E S E N S E
H ■ L ■ P ■ Q ■ I ■ A ■ L ■ ■
E L E G I S T ■ U N T W I N E
S ■ M ■ N ■ I ■ I ■ T ■ L ■ V
P R A C T I C A L ■ I R E N E
I ■ T ■ H ■ L ■ ■ ■ N ■ D ■ N
A L I C E S P R I N G S ■ ■ ■
N ■ S ■ P ■ O ■ O ■ P ■ P ■ E
■ ■ ■ S I T T I N G R O O M S
M ■ P ■ P ■ E ■ ■ E ■ T ■ O ■
A B O V E ■ N I G H T S P O T
R ■ G ■ L ■ T ■ A ■ T ■ L ■ E
M A R T I N I ■ M A Y F A I R
O ■ O ■ N ■ A ■ I ■ ■ N ■ I ■
T I M B E R L I N E ■ O T I C
```

25

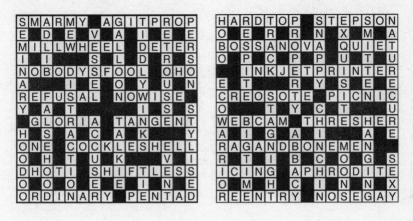

```
S M A R M Y   A G I T P R O P
E D   E V A   I E     E E
M I L L W H E E L   D E T E R
I   I   S   L   D R S
N O B O D Y S F O O L   O H O
A     I E   O Y   U N
R E F U S A L   N O W I S E
Y   A T       I S S
  G L O R I A   T A N G E N T
H   S   A C   A K       Y
O N E   C O C K L E S H E L L
O   H   T U   K   V   I
D H O T I   S H I F T L E S S
O   O   O   E E   I N E
O R D I N A R Y   P E N T A D
```

26

```
H A R D T O P   S T E P S O N
O   E   R R   N X   M   A
B O S S A N O V A   Q U I E T
O   P   C P   P U   T   U
    I N K J E T P R I N T E R
E   T   R Y   S E     E
C R E O S O T E   P I C N I C
O     T   Y C   T   U
W E B C A M   T H R E S H E R
A   I   G A   I   A     E
R A G A N D B O N E M E N
R   T   I B   C O   G   S
I C I N G   A P H R O D I T E
O   M   H C   I   N   N   X
R E E N T R Y   N O S E G A Y
```

27

```
C A L I P H   T H E I D I O T
H   I   O     O M   N   O
I N V E R S E   R E B E C C A
N   I   T     A A   I E D
S E D E R   M A T T B U S B Y
T     A   O   I   E S
R U G B Y U N I O N   W A I F
A   E   S D   N H   N   I
P I T T   B E N E F A C T O R
    A   T V   L   S   E
P A R T I S A N S   T A M I L
E   O   R L   O   I A   I
R O U L A D E   N A N K I N G
C   N   N R   G   N   H
H I D E A W A Y   A S C E N T
```

28

```
S C A P A F L O W   V O C A B
I   S   N A   A A   A   U
G E T O N E S S K A T E S O N
M   U   O H   E F   T   N
A R D O U R   M U T U A L L Y
Y   N   A P   L E   G
S W I T C H B A C K   A S T I
C   N   E O   A E   I   R
A P S E   S U B L I M I N A L
L   C   Q T   L   B   T
L E A D U P T O   B R A H M A
Y   R   A U   Z A   E   P
W A L L S T R E E T C R A S H
A   E   A N   B E   I   I
G A T O R   S H U D D E R E D
```

SOLUTIONS

29

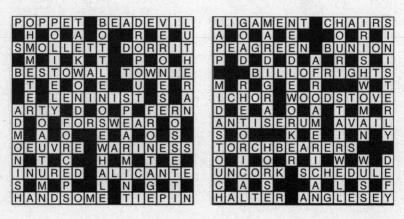

```
P O P P E T   B E A D E V I L
  H   O   A   O   R   E   U
S M O L L E T T   D O R R I T
  M   I   K   T   P   O   H
B E S T O W A L   T O W N I E
  T   E   O   E   U   E   R
  E   L E N I N I S T   S   A
A R T Y   D   O   P   F E R N
D   O   F O R S W E A R   O S
M   A   O   E   A   O   S
O E U V R E   W A R I N E S S
N   T   C   H   M   T   E
I N U R E D   A L I C A N T E
S   M   P   L   N   G   T
H A N D S O M E   T I E P I N
```

30

```
L I G A M E N T   C H A I R S
A   O   A   E   O   R   I
P E A G R E E N   B U N I O N
P   D   D D   A   R   S   I
    B I L L O F R I G H T S
M   R   G   E   R   W   T
I C H O R   W O O D S T O V E
D   E   A   O   A   T   M   R
A N T I S E R U M   A V A I L
S   O   K   E   I   N   Y
T O R C H B E A R E R S
O   I   O   R   I   W   W   D
U N C O R K   S C H E D U L E
C   A   S   A   L   S   F
H A L T E R   A N G L E S E Y
```

31

```
A L L I M P O R T A N T
R   O   Y   N A U F S
C Y C L E   C O L U M N I S T
H   A   Y   O   E   B L I
W A L L E D U P   W E L L I N
A   A   R   R   I G
Y O U N G E S T   R O D N E Y
  T   R   E   S   N G
C A H I E R   C A R E S S E D
U   O   N   L     T I
P A R K A S   S T A L B A N S
T   I D   S B E T   E
I N T R I C A T E   V O I L A
E Y   A K E   E   O S
  I N D I F F E R E N C E
```

32

```
C O N T R A R Y   A G N A T E
O   A   O   U   O   O   U   R
U L U R U   B A N D W A G O N
R   R   N   Y E   I   U   E
T H U N D E R E D   T U S K S
I   S   E   G H   T   T
E A R T H E D   E X O T I C
R   E   O   U   N   H
  A D J U S T   B Y T H E B Y
U   L L   A   R S   D
T W E E D   L O O K A F T E R
A   T E K   W Y   W   O
H I T O R M I S S   I C I N G
A   E   E E E   E N   X   E
N E R U D A   F R I G H T E N
```

33

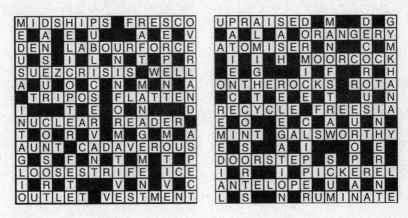

M	I	D	S	H	I	P	S		F	R	E	S	C	O
E		A		E		U			A		E		V	
D	E	N		L	A	B	O	U	R	F	O	R	C	E
U		S		I		L		N		T		P		R
S	U	E	Z	C	R	I	S	I	S		W	E	L	L
A		U		O		C		N		M		N		A
	T	R	I	P	O	S		F	L	A	T	T	E	N
I			T		E		O		N			D		
N	U	C	L	E	A	R		R	E	A	D	E	R	
T		O		R		V		M		G		M		A
A	U	N	T		C	A	D	A	V	E	R	O	U	S
G		S		F		N		T		M		T		P
L	O	O	S	E	S	T	R	I	F	E		I	C	E
I		R		T			V		N		V		C	
O	U	T	L	E	T		V	E	S	T	M	E	N	T

34

U	P	R	A	I	S	E	D		M		D		G
	A		L		A		O	R	A	N	G	E	R	Y
A	T	O	M	I	S	E	R		N		C		M
	I		I		H		M	O	O	R	C	O	C	K
	E		G			F		F		R		H	
O	N	T	H	E	R	O	C	K	S		R	O	T	A
	C		T		E		E		T		U		N
R	E	C	Y	C	L	E		F	R	E	E	S	I	A
E		O		E		C		A		U		N	
M	I	N	T		G	A	L	S	W	O	R	T	H	Y
E		S		A		I			O			E	
D	O	O	R	S	T	E	P		S		P		R
I		R		I			P	I	C	K	E	R	E	L
A	N	T	E	L	O	P	E		U		A		N
L		S		N		R	U	M	I	N	A	T	E

35

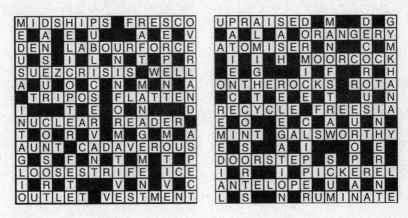

S	P	A	R	K	L	E	R		D	I	W	A	L	I
	R		I		E		O		E		A		O	
L	O	N	G		V	O	C	I	F	E	R	O	U	S
	P		O		E			E		D		G		
R	E	P	U	B	L	I	C	A	N		O	A	H	U
L		R			A		S		F					
A	L	A	S	T	A	I	R		I	N	F	A	M	Y
E			L		R		V					E		
G	R	A	V	E	L		O	P	E	N	F	I	R	E
	E		E		L			L			I		C	
S	P	A	R		V	O	L	U	M	I	N	O	U	S
	L		A		I			I			E		R	
G	A	I	N	S	A	Y	I	N	G		A	K	I	N
	I		D		T		N		H		R		A	
I	N	C	A	S	E		N	O	T	A	T	A	L	L

36

B	E	T	R	A	Y		S	P	L	E	N	D	I	D
A		U		N			H		M		I			R
R	E	D	R	E	S	S		I	M	P	A	S	T	O
E		O		C		W		L		L		P		V
F	A	R	A	D		E	L	A	B	O	R	A	T	E
A			O		E		N		Y			R		
C	O	N	S	T	I	T	U	T	E		L	A	M	B
E		U		E		N		H		P		G		U
D	E	M	O		T	O	U	R	N	A	M	E	N	T
		E		L		T		O		S			T	
H	O	R	S	E	W	H	I	P		T	A	S	T	E
O		A		T		I		I		I		O		H
K	I	T	C	H	E	N		C	A	R	D	I	F	F
U		O		A		G				A		R		L
M	O	R	A	L	I	S	T		F	L	U	K	E	Y

37

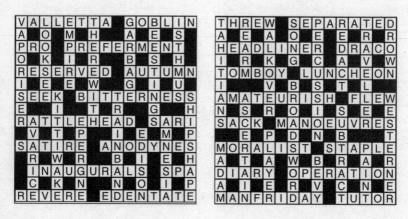

V	A	L	L	E	T	T	A		G	O	B	L	I	N
A		O		M		H		A		E		S		
P	R	O		P	R	E	F	E	R	M	E	N	T	
O		K		I		R		B		S		H		
R	E	S	E	R	V	E	D		A	U	T	U	M	N
I		E		E		W		G		I		U		
S	E	E	K		B	I	T	T	E	R	N	E	S	S
E			I		T		R		G			H		
R	A	T	T	L	E	H	E	A	D		S	A	R	I
	V		T		P		I		E		M		P	
S	A	T	I	R	E		A	N	O	D	Y	N	E	S
	R		W		R		B		I		E		H	
	I	N	A	U	G	U	R	A	L	S		S	P	A
	C		K		N			N		O		I		P
R	E	V	E	R	E		E	D	E	N	T	A	T	E

38

T	H	R	E	W		S	E	P	A	R	A	T	E	D
A		E		A		O		E		E		R		R
H	E	A	D	L	I	N	E	R		D	R	A	C	O
I		R		K		G		C		A		V		W
T	O	M	B	O	Y		L	U	N	C	H	E	O	N
I			V		B		S		T		L		N	
A	M	A	T	E	U	R	I	S	H		F	L	E	W
N		S		R		O		I		S		E		E
S	A	C	K		M	A	N	O	E	U	V	R	E	S
	E		P		D		N		B			T		
M	O	R	A	L	I	S	T		S	T	A	P	L	E
A		T		A		W		B		R		A		R
D	I	A	R	Y		O	P	E	R	A	T	I	O	N
A		I		E		R		V		C		N		E
M	A	N	F	R	I	D	A	Y		T	U	T	O	R

39

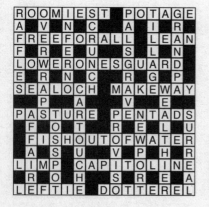

R	O	O	M	I	E	S	T		P	O	T	A	G	E
A		V		N		C		A		I		R		
F	R	E	E	F	O	R	A	L	L		L	E	A	N
F		R		E		U		S		L		N		
L	O	W	E	R	O	N	E	S	G	U	A	R	D	
E		R		N		C		R		G		P		
S	E	A	L	O	C	H		M	A	K	E	W	A	Y
		P		A			V		E					
P	A	S	T	U	R	E		P	E	N	T	A	D	S
	F		O		T		R		L		U			
	F	I	S	H	O	U	T	O	F	W	A	T	E	R
	A		S		U		V		P		H		R	
L	I	M	P		C	A	P	I	T	O	L	I	N	E
	R		O		H		S		R		E		A	
L	E	F	T	I	E		D	O	T	T	E	R	E	L

40

S	T	O	O	P		F	L	O	U	R	I	S	H	
A		R		O		R		V		O		H		
H	E	A	V	I	S	I	D	E	L	A	Y	E	R	
A		N		N		D		R		S		A		C
R	I	G	H	T	H	A	N	D		T	Y	R	O	L
A			L		Y		O			L			O	
D	U	L	C	E	T		I	N	D	I	G	E	N	T
E		A		S		H		E		R		G		H
S	I	N	I	S	T	E	R		M	O	U	S	S	E
E		D			A		D		N			S		
R	I	G	E	L		T	A	O	I	S	E	A	C	H
T		R		A		W		R		T		C		O
	C	A	R	T	R	A	N	S	P	O	R	T	E	R
	V		H		V		E		N		O			S
R	E	G	I	M	E	N	T		E	R	N	I	E	

41

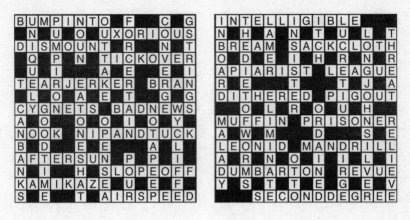

42

43

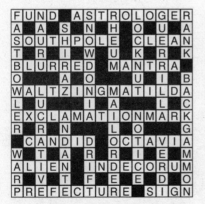

44

SOLUTIONS

45

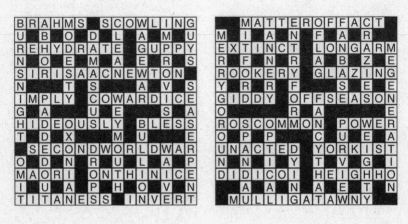

46

47

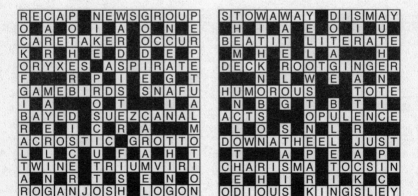

48

49

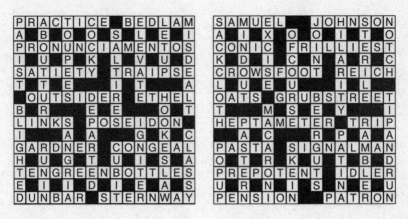

```
P R A C T I C E ■ B E D L A M
A ■ B ■ O ■ O ■ S ■ L ■ E ■ I
A P R O N U N C I A M E N T O S
I ■ U ■ P ■ K ■ L ■ V ■ U ■ D
S A T I E T Y ■ T R A I P S E
T ■ T ■ E ■ I ■ T ■ ■ ■ A
■ O U T S I D E R ■ E T H E L
B ■ R ■ E ■ E ■ ■ ■ O ■ T
L I N K S ■ P O S E I D O N ■
I ■ ■ A ■ A ■ G ■ K ■ C
G A R D N E R ■ C O N G E A L
H ■ U ■ G ■ T ■ U ■ I ■ S ■ A
T E N G R E E N B O T T L E S
E ■ I ■ I ■ D ■ I ■ E ■ A ■ S
D U N B A R ■ S T E R N W A Y
```

50

```
S A M U E L ■ J O H N S O N
A ■ I ■ X ■ O ■ O ■ I ■ T ■ O
C O N I C ■ F R I L L I E S T
K ■ D ■ I ■ C ■ N ■ A ■ R ■ C
C R O W S F O O T ■ R E I C H
L ■ U ■ E ■ U ■ ■ ■ I ■ L
O A T S ■ G R U B S T R E E T
T ■ M ■ S ■ E ■ Y ■ ■ ■ I
H E P T A M E T E R ■ T R I P
■ A ■ C ■ ■ ■ R ■ P ■ A ■ A
P A S T A ■ S I G N A L M A N
O ■ T ■ R ■ K ■ U ■ T ■ B ■ D
P R E P O T E N T ■ I D L E R
U ■ R ■ N ■ I ■ S ■ N ■ E ■ U
P E N S I O N ■ P A T R O N
```

51

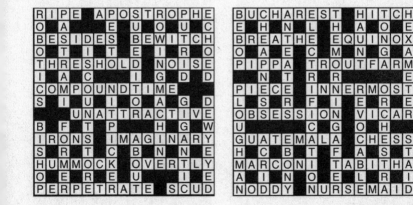

```
R I P E ■ A P O S T R O P H E
O ■ A ■ E ■ U ■ O ■ U ■ C
B E S I D E S ■ B E W I T C H
O ■ T ■ I ■ T ■ E ■ I ■ R ■ O
T H R E S H O L D ■ N O I S E
I ■ A ■ C ■ I ■ G ■ D ■ D
C O M P O U N D T I M E ■ ■
S ■ I ■ U ■ I ■ O ■ A ■ G ■ D
■ U N A T T R A C T I V E
B ■ F ■ T ■ P ■ H ■ G ■ W
I R O N S ■ I M A G I N A R Y
S ■ R ■ T ■ C ■ B ■ N ■ N ■ E
H U M M O C K ■ O V E R T L Y
O ■ E ■ R ■ E ■ U ■ ■ I ■ E
P E R P E T R A T E ■ S C U D
```

52

```
B U C H A R E S T ■ H I T C H
E ■ H ■ N ■ L ■ H ■ A ■ O ■ E
B R E A T H E ■ E Q U I N O X
O ■ A ■ E ■ C ■ M ■ N ■ G ■ A
P I P P A ■ T R O U T F A R M
■ N ■ T ■ R ■ R ■ ■ ■ E
P I E C E ■ I N N E R M O S T
L ■ S ■ R ■ F ■ I ■ E ■ R ■ E
O B S E S S I O N ■ V I C A R
U ■ ■ ■ C ■ G ■ O ■ H
G U A T E M A L A ■ C H E S S
H ■ C ■ B ■ T ■ F ■ A ■ S ■ T
M A R C O N I ■ T A B I T H A
A ■ I ■ N ■ O ■ E ■ L ■ R ■ I
N O D D Y ■ N U R S E M A I D
```

SOLUTIONS

53

```
V A M P I S H   W R I T E U P
A   U   M   A   E   M   G   R
M A R   P U R P L E P R O S E
O   I   A   D   L   O       S
O N E T R A C K   R U M B L E
S   L   T   H   M   N   U   L
E A S T   P E R I O D I C A L
    P   T   E   N   S   K
L E A D E R S H I P   B R I E
I   R   N   E   B   A   A   N
B I K I N G   B U T T E R E D
E     Y   N   D   O   E   O
R O D E S H O T G U N   B A R
I   O   O   U   E   C   I   S
A C C E N T S   T H E A T R E
```

54

```
W I L M S L O W   E S C A P E
  M   U   I   A   U   U   E
  A D M I N I S T R A T O R
  G   S   G   S   I       U
B I S T R O   A P P R A I S E
  S   H     I   I   U   A
I M P E R I L L E D   C O L E
    W   M     E   O
E B R O   P L E A S A N T R Y
  E   R   R   F     T   A
H A N D C U F F   S T R I V E
  R   D   A   E   A   A
C O N D E S C E N D I N G
  A   E   N   E   N   R   E
S T R E E T   D E A D E N D S
```

55

```
A L B A N Y   A D V A N C E D
P   U   E   E   R   R   I   A
A B D O M E N   A R C A N U M
R   G   O   D   U   H   N   N
T E E M   P I L G R I M A G E
    T   D   V   H   T     D
P L A C E M E N T   R U P E E
E   R   A       A   I   S
D R Y A D   S L E E V E N U T
O       L   N   L   E   E
M E T R O P O L I S   L A M P
E   A   C   W   J   A   P   O
T R I C K E D   A L C O P O P
E   L   E   O   H   N   L   P
R E S I D E N T   H E R E S Y
```

56

```
B A R B A D O S   E     A   C
  M   O   A   A N G L E S E Y
L A I R   N   N   G   H   C
  R   D I N G D O N G B E L L
  E   E   Y   B   O   U   A
A T H R O B   A N G S T R O M
  T   C   O   G     T   E
T O P O N Y M   R O B E S O N
O   L     W   C   R   R
P H Y L L I D A   O F F P A T
T   I   N   X   N   L   C
A P R E T T Y P E N N Y   U
B   I   U   A   E   N U L L
L A N D F I L L   L   U   A
E   K   T   M I L I T A R Y
```

57

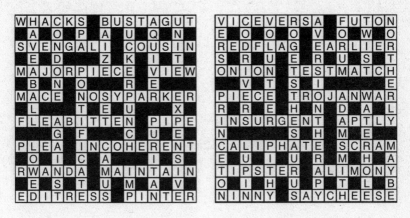

58

59

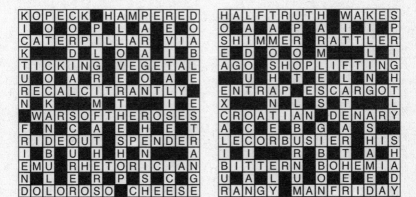

60

61

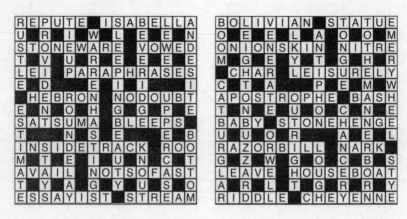

```
R E P U T E   I S A B E L L A
U R   I   W   L   E   E     N
S T O N E W A R E   V O W E D
T   V   U   R   E   E   E   E
L E I   P A R A P H R A S E S
E D   E   I   I           I
  H E B R O N   N O D O U B T
E   N   O   H   G   G   P   E
S A T S U M A   B L E E P S
T     N   S   E       E     B
I N S I D E T R A C K   R O O
M   T   E   I   U   N   C   T
A V A I L   N O T S O F A S T
T   Y   A   G   Y   U   S   O
E S S A Y I S T   S T R E A M
```

62

```
B O L I V I A N   S T A T U E
O   E   E   L   A   O   O   M
O N I O N S K I N   N I T R E
M   G   E   Y   T   G   H   R
  C H A R   L E I S U R E L Y
C   T   A   P   E   M   W
A P O S T R O P H E   B A S H
T   N   E   U   O   C   N   E
B A B Y   S T O N E H E N G E
U   U   O   R     A   E   L
R A Z O R B I L L   N A R K
G   Z   W   G   O   C   B   S
L E A V E   H O U S E B O A T
A   R   L   T   G   R   R   Y
R I D D L E   C H E Y E N N E
```

63

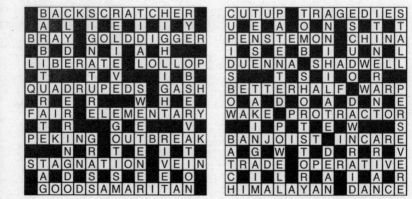

```
  B A C K S C R A T C H E R
  A   I   E   I   I   Y
B R A Y   G O L D D I G G E R
  B   D   N   I   A   H
L I B E R A T E   L O L L O P
  T     T   V     I   B
Q U A D R U P E D S   G A S H
R   E   R   W   H   E
F A I R   E L E M E N T A R Y
  T   R     G   E   V
P E K I N G   O U T B R E A K
    N   R   T   E   I   T
S T A G N A T I O N   V E I N
  A   D   S   S   E   E   O
G O O D S A M A R I T A N
```

64

```
C U T U P   T R A G E D I E S
U   E   A   O   N   S   T   T
P E N S T E M O N   C H I N A
I   S   E   B   I   U   N   L
D U E N N A   S H A D W E L L
S     T   S   I   O   R
B E T T E R H A L F   W A R P
O   A   D   O   A   D   N   E
W A K E   P R O T R A C T O R
  I   P   T   E   W       S
B A N J O I S T   I N C A R E
A   G   W   T   D   R   R   V
T R A D E   O P E R A T I V E
C   I   L   R   A   I   A   R
H I M A L A Y A N   D A N C E
```

65

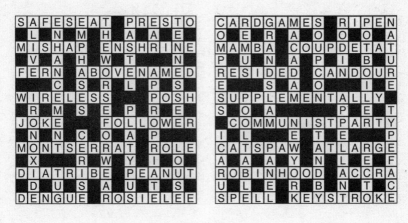

S	A	F	E	S	E	A	T		P	R	E	S	T	O
	L		N		M		H		A		A		E	
M	I	S	H	A	P		E	N	S	H	R	I	N	E
	V		A		H		W		T				N	
F	E	R	N		A	B	O	V	E	N	A	M	E	D
		C		S		R		L		P		S		
W	I	R	E	L	E	S	S		P	O	S	H		
	R		M		S		E		R		E			
J	O	K	E		F	O	L	L	O	W	E	R		
	N		N		C		O		A		P			
M	O	N	T	S	E	R	R	A	T		R	O	L	E
	X			R		W		Y		I		O		
D	I	A	T	R	I	B	E		P	E	A	N	U	T
	D		U		S		A		U		T		S	
D	E	N	G	U	E		R	O	S	I	E	L	E	E

66

C	A	R	D	G	A	M	E	S		R	I	P	E	N
O		E	R		A		O		O		O		A	
M	A	M	B	A		C	O	U	P	D	E	T	A	T
P		U		N		A		P		I		B		U
R	E	S	I	D	E	D		C	A	N	D	O	U	R
E				S		A		O			I			E
S	U	P	P	L	E	M	E	N	T	A	L	L	Y	
S		O		A					P		E	T		
	C	O	M	M	U	N	I	S	T	P	A	R	T	Y
I		L			E		T		E				P	
C	A	T	S	P	A	W		A	T	L	A	R	G	E
A		A		A		Y		N		L		E		F
R	O	B	I	N	H	O	O	D		A	C	C	R	A
U		L		E		R		B		N		T		C
S	P	E	L	L		K	E	Y	S	T	R	O	K	E

67

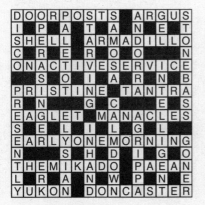

D	O	O	R	P	O	S	T	S		A	R	G	U	S
I		P		A		T		A		N		E		T
S	H	E	L	L		A	R	M	A	D	I	L	L	O
C		R		E		R		O		O				N
O	N	A	C	T	I	V	E	S	E	R	V	I	C	E
		S		O		I		A		R		N		B
P	R	I	S	T	I	N	E		T	A	N	T	R	A
R		N		G		C		E				E		S
E	A	G	L	E	T		M	A	N	A	C	L	E	S
S		E		L		I		L	G	L				
E	A	R	L	Y	O	N	E	M	O	R	N	I	N	G
N			S		H		D		I		G			O
T	H	E	M	I	K	A	D	O		P	A	E	A	N
L		R		A		N		W		P		N		E
Y	U	K	O	N		D	O	N	C	A	S	T	E	R

68

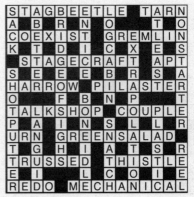

S	T	A	G	B	E	E	T	L	E		T	A	R	N
A		B		R		N		O			O		T	O
C	O	E	X	I	S	T		G	R	E	M	L	I	N
K		T		D		I		C		X		E		S
	S	T	A	G	E	C	R	A	F	T		A	P	T
S		E		E		E		B		R		S		A
H	A	R	R	O	W		P	I	L	A	S	T	E	R
O			F		B		N		P					T
T	A	L	K	S	H	O	P		C	O	U	P	L	E
P		A		I		N		S		L	L			R
U	R	N		G	R	E	E	N	S	A	L	A	D	
T		G		H		I		A		T		S		R
T	R	U	S	S	E	D		T	H	I	S	T	L	E
E		I				L		C		O		I		E
R	E	D	O		M	E	C	H	A	N	I	C	A	L

SOLUTIONS

69

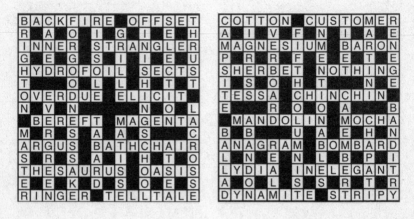

```
B A C K F I R E ■ O F F S E T
R ■ A ■ O ■ I ■ G ■ I ■ E ■ H
I N N E R ■ S T R A N G L E R
G ■ E ■ G ■ S ■ I ■ I ■ E ■ U
H Y D R O F O I L ■ S E C T S
T ■ ■ O ■ L ■ L ■ H ■ T ■ T ■
O V E R D U E ■ E L I C I T ■
N ■ V ■ N ■ ■ ■ N ■ O ■ L ■ ■
■ B E R E F T ■ M A G E N T A
M ■ R ■ S ■ A ■ A ■ S ■ ■ C ■
A R G U S ■ B A T H C H A I R
S ■ R ■ S ■ A ■ I ■ H ■ T ■ O
T H E S A U R U S ■ O A S I S
E ■ E ■ K ■ D ■ S ■ O ■ E ■ S
R I N G E R ■ T E L L T A L E
```

70

```
C O T T O N ■ C U S T O M E R
A ■ I ■ V ■ F ■ N ■ I ■ A ■ E
M A G N E S I U M ■ B A R O N
P ■ R ■ R ■ F ■ E ■ E ■ T ■ E
S H E R B E T ■ N O T H I N G
I ■ S ■ O ■ H ■ T ■ N ■ E ■ ■
T E S S A ■ C H I N C H I N ■
E ■ ■ R ■ O ■ O ■ A ■ ■ ■ B
■ M A N D O L I N ■ M O C H A
B ■ B ■ U ■ A ■ E ■ H ■ ■ N
A N A G R A M ■ B O M B A R D
L ■ N ■ E ■ N ■ L ■ B ■ P ■ I
L Y D I A ■ I N E L E G A N T
A ■ O ■ L ■ S ■ S ■ R ■ T ■ R
D Y N A M I T E ■ S T R I P Y
```

71

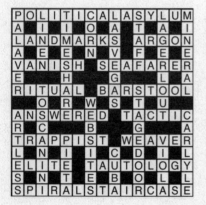

```
P O L I T I C A L A S Y L U M
A ■ I ■ I ■ O ■ A ■ T ■ A ■ I
L A N D M A R K S ■ A R G O N
A ■ E ■ E ■ N ■ V ■ F ■ E ■ E
V A N I S H ■ S E A F A R E R
E ■ ■ H ■ ■ G ■ ■ ■ L ■ ■ A
R I T U A L ■ B A R S T O O L
■ O ■ R ■ W ■ S ■ T ■ U ■ ■
A N S W E R E D ■ T A C T I C
R ■ C ■ ■ B ■ ■ G ■ ■ ■ A
T R A P P I S T ■ W E A V E R
L ■ N ■ I ■ I ■ C ■ D ■ I ■ L
E L I T E ■ T A U T O L O G Y
S ■ N ■ T ■ E ■ B ■ O ■ L ■ L
S P I R A L S T A I R C A S E
```

72

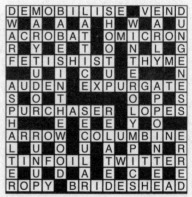

```
D E M O B I L I S E ■ V E N D
W ■ A ■ A ■ A ■ H ■ W ■ A ■ U
A C R O B A T ■ O M I C R O N
R ■ Y ■ E ■ T ■ O ■ N ■ L ■ G
F E T I S H I S T ■ T H Y M E
■ U ■ I ■ C ■ U ■ E ■ ■ N ■
A U D E N ■ E X P U R G A T E
S ■ O ■ T ■ ■ O ■ P ■ S ■
P U R C H A S E R ■ L O P E S
H ■ ■ E ■ E ■ E ■ Y ■ O ■
A R R O W ■ C O L U M B I N E
L ■ U ■ O ■ U ■ A ■ P ■ N ■ R
T I N F O I L ■ T W I T T E R
E ■ U ■ D ■ A ■ E ■ C ■ E ■ E
R O P Y ■ B R I D E S H E A D
```

73

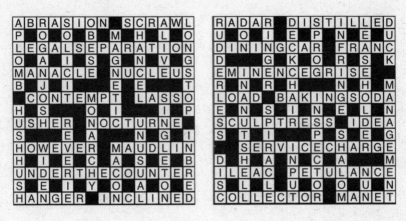

```
A B R A S I O N   S C R A W L
P   O O   B   M   H   L     O
L E G A L S E P A R A T I O N
O   A   I   S   G   N   V   G
M A N A C L E   N U C L E U S
B   J   I     E   E   E     T
  C O N T E M P T   L A S S O
H   S     O   I       I     P
U S H E R   N O C T U R N E
S   E     A     N   G     I
H O W E V E R   M A U D L I N
H   I   E   C   A   S   E   B
U N D E R T H E C O U N T E R
S   E   I   Y   O   A   O   E
H A N G E R   I N C L I N E D
```

74

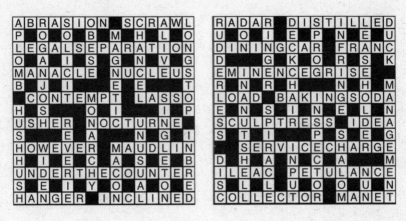

```
R A D A R   D I S T I L L E D
U   O I   E   P   N   E     U
D I N I N G C A R   F R A N C
D   G   K   O   R   S     K
E M I N E N C E G R I S E
R   N   R H   N   H   M
L O A D   B A K I N G S O D A
E   N   S I N   E   L     N
S C U L P T R E S S   I D E A
S   T     I   P   S   E   G
  S E R V I C E C H A R G E
D   H   A N   C   A     M
I L E A C   P E T U L A N C E
S   L   L   U   O   O   U N
C O L L E C T O R   M A N E T
```

75

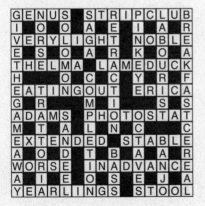

```
G E N U S   S T R I P C L U B
I   O O   A E   I   A     R
V E R Y L I G H T   N O B L E
E   S O   A   R   K   O     A
T H E L M A   L A M E D U C K
H   O     C   C   Y   R   F
E A T I N G O U T   E R I C A
G   R     M   I       S   S
A D A M S   P H O T O S T A T
M   T     A   L   N   C     C
E X T E N D E D   S T A B L E
A   O   D   T   B   A   A   R
W O R S E   I N A D V A N C E
A   I   E   O   S   E   J   A
Y E A R L I N G S   S T O O L
```

76

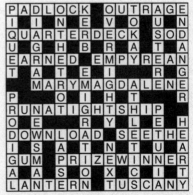

```
P A D L O C K   O U T R A G E
I   I   N   E   V   O   U   N
Q U A R T E R D E C K   S O D
U   G   H   B   R   A     A
E A R N E D   E M P Y R E A N
T   A   T   E   I       R   G
  M A R Y M A G D A L E N E
P   O   I   H   T       R
R U N A T I G H T S H I P
O   E   R   Y   L   E     H
D O W N L O A D   S E E T H E
I   S   A   T   N   T   U   A
G U M   P R I Z E W I N N E R
A   A   S   O   X   C   I   T
L A N T E R N   T U S C A N Y
```

SOLUTIONS

77

```
B O W W O W   I S O T H E R M
O   A   M   B   T   O   P   A
B A L L A D E E R   L A S E R
C   L   N   E   I   E   O   I
A S P   I N F A N T R Y M A N
T   A     W   G   A     A
  S P A R S E   O N B O A R D
S   E   A   L   F   L   L   E
C A R A C A L   P R E F A B
A     E   I   E     B     C
F A R T H I N G A L E   A S H
F   A   O   G   R   M   S   E
O T T E R   T E L E M E T E R
L   E   S   O   S   E   E   R
D A L S E G N O   S T O R E Y
```

78

```
S W A L L O W   C O M I C A L
U   S   I   A   A   E   L   E
P O T B O I L E R   M O U R N
P   O   N   K   V   E   N   G
L O U S E   O V E R N I G H T
Y   N   S   N   T       H
    D I S P A S S I O N A T E
P   E   I   O     R     N
I N D U S T R I A L I S T
N   A   P   N   I   P
P O R T F O L I O   F A L S E
O   A   F   U   P   E   L   D
I N C U R   S P E A R H E A D
N   E   O   T   R   N   R   L
T Y R A N N Y   A N O D Y N E
```

79

```
K I S S A G R A M   S T A F F
E   H   R   A   U   H   T   L
B I O M A S S   T W I T C H Y
A   O   C   P   A   V   L   W
B O T C H   U P T H E P O L E
    F   N   T   E   R   S   I
S A R D I N I A     B E R G
A   O   D   N   G   A   Q   H
L I M O   J U M P S U I T
E   T   B   A   N   P   A
S C H O O L B A G   L O R D S
T   E   W   J   A   E   T   H
A T H L O N E   D I P T E R A
L   I   U   C   I   I   R   M
K A P U T   T E N N E S S E E
```

80

```
C O N S O L E   G L A S G O W
L   A   B   U   A   V   A   I
A N T I V I R U S   O R M E R
U   U   I   O     I   B   E
S Y R I A   F I E L D G O A L
E   A   T   I   C   G   E
  F L Y I N G F O R T R E S S
F   O   H   F   H       S
E N F A N T T E R R I B L E
S   O   E   I   G   A   S
S U R C H A R G E   H A R E M
E   G   I   N   B   W   O
D R O O P   A U D I O B O O K
U   O   P   S   L   N   O   E
P A D D O C K   Y I E L D E D
```